UNPLUGGED

UNPLUGGED

How Organizations Lose Their Energy and How to Get It Back

Steve Buchholz and Tom Roth
Wilson Learning Worldwide Inc.

WILSON LEARNING CORPORATION

Wilson Learning Corporation
8000 W. 78th Street, Suite 200
Edina, MN 55439
800.328.7937
WilsonLearning.com

© Wilson Learning Worldwide Inc.

© 2019 Wilson Learning Worldwide Inc.

Printed in the United States of America

ISBN-13: 978-1-73272-770-0

Dedication

We dedicate this book to Steve's wife Deb, and children Peter and Molly, and to Tom's wife Pam, and children Christopher and Geoffrey, for their unique and unwavering support.

Contents

Contents

Foreword

By my twenties, I swear I was traveling like an airline pilot and reading more than a big city newspaper editor. I'd joined a small-yet-bustling, family-owned management consultancy in 1992 with twenty facilitators and a half-dozen instructional designers. It was trial by fire, but I treasured it for what it *really* was: a white-hot crucible that might refine precious metals, be they worldly clients or we rough-around-the-edges punks who served them.

To accumulate practical knowledge, skills, and activities we thought might bring value to actual participants in leadership workshops, strategy sessions, and interpersonal courses we offered at the time, our entire team read everything we could get our hands on. This included managerial staples by the likes of Peter Drucker, Ken Blanchard, Michael Porter, Alvin Toffler, George Land, Warren Bennis, Charles Handy, David Bradford, Allan Cohen, Peter Koestenbaum, Paul Hersey, Tom Peters, and Eliyahu Goldratt (whose groundbreaking work, *The Goal*, was one of the first and best storybooks about business that virtually anyone had ever read, preceding Patrick Lencioni's popularity by nearly two decades). I was also exploring those whose work was just gaining international momentum at the time: Peter Senge, Gary Hamel, Kenichi Ohmae, Rosabeth Moss Kanter, Jon Katzenbach, Richard Leider, and Stephen Covey among them.

Simultaneously, as a fortunate licensee of Wilson Learning, our tiny dinghy of an organization was the recipient of a virtual boatload of world-class resources, there seemingly being no end to the solutions at our fingertips through our association with the company. These included organization development curricula and programs with delightfully sticky titles like *Leading in Challenging Times, Leading From Within, The Leader-Manager, High-Performance Team Workshop, Counselor Salesperson, Consulting with Clients, Advanced Account Management, Signature Service,* and everyone's perennial favorite (and global bestseller) *Managing Interpersonal Relationships (Social Styles).* By 1993, one year after I'd begun my nascent career, I was attending one of Wilson Learning's incomparable conferences (frequently held in hubs like Minneapolis, Orlando, or Chicago) and getting exposure to unparalleled panels, people, and literally more on-point research than I'd experienced in seven years of college. It was at one of these early conferences (an embarrassment of riches) that I first met Tom Roth and Steve Buchholz.

Tom was a riveting and accessible storyteller, and I remember my twenty-something-self thinking, *Man, this guy is so polished.* On the one hand, he came across as what a colleague had hitherto described as "a silver-haired CEO," but he also had this easy, innate ability to draw one in—like a great, dyed-in-the-wool Midwesterner spinning yarns and telling stories on his porch at dusk—then beaning you right between the eyes with some glistening pearl of wisdom that no one saw coming.

Following Tom's outstanding morning presentation (which had occurred in a ballroom), I eagerly awaited an intimate afternoon session to be presented by Steve Buchholz.

Now, I know it's hard to imagine this (so you'll have to join me in the Way Back Machine), but this was the era just *before* the Internet, so I had never even laid eyes on Steve's face. I only knew him through writing and reputation, both of which were every bit as strong as Tom's. I was familiar with Steve's 1976 doctoral dissertation, *The Effects of Training in Managing Interpersonal Relationships on the Perceptions of Social Style* because—when considered alongside the work of contemporaries like Brad and Velma Lashbrook—it was among the more noteworthy recent contributions describing the utilitarian value of social science in the workplace.

In the intervening years since my first exposure to Steve that afternoon—and his beautifully delivered presentation (more Socratic Method/ *dialogue* than *monologue*)—I have come to know him quite well, come to know his story very well, and come to appreciate Tom and him evermore.

Proceeding from Vice President of Research and Development at Wilson Learning to co-authoring 1987's seminal *Creating the High-Performance Team* (with Tom) and the renowned *Aftershock: Helping People through Corporate Change* (with Harry Woodward), Steve has grown from a rather quiet and unassuming (if not wholly central) figure at the heart of virtually every early-era Wilson Learning success to become one of the world's most sought-after subject matter experts on human energy and interaction in the workplace. As I write this, in fact—hand to God—I have literally just forwarded him a request to speak on the topic of corporate change and human energy for Saudi Aramco, the world's largest energy company. (This giggle-worthy irony is not lost on me—and I hope it's not lost on you, either—the first time I met Steve his question to me being, "I'm in the *energy* business. What do *you* do?")

In fact, to illuminate his reputation all the more, allow me another anecdote: I remember being in San Francisco in 1995 or 1996, having dinner along the pier with a college buddy and telling him I'd seen Steve speak in Minneapolis just a year or two prior, and my friend clarifying, "*The* Steve Buchholz? The *Aftershock* guy?"

"Yep, one and the same."

"Wow," he said.

Wow is right.

In 1997, Steve kindly agreed to participate as a reader on my doctoral committee, my dissertation zeroing-in on workplace involvement (one delightful finding being the seemingly paradoxical nature of employee involvement: The more one *includes* employees in meaningful work, the likelier their *buy-in* to organizational change, the greater their *personal and professional fulfillment* and—drumroll, here—*the higher their energy*, both at work *and* at home). At first blush it might seem counterintuitive that the more we include employees in additional work, the more and harder they work, but it's the rule, not the exception, and especially if it's meaningful. We *all* aspire to be part of something worthwhile—do we not—so why should the workplace be any different? Indeed, it's not. More to the point, assuming an employee works approximately 2,080 hours/year (not an atypical number for Americans) for forty-three years (a common minimal duration, ages twenty-two to sixty-five being the acceptable least), he or she spends a whopping 89,440 hours away from family and friends! To the extent one includes employees in meaningful activities, then he or she just might have the great gift of watching a job become a career and perhaps even a vocation (the root of this final word being *vocare*, the Latin for "to call, to summon", aka, a calling). What a powerful journey this can be, and one that Ralph Waldo Emerson understood personally when he wrote the words, "The crowning fortune of a man is to be born to some pursuit which finds him employment *and* happiness, whether it be to make baskets, or broadswords, or canals, or statues, or songs."

I appreciate that "employee engagement" is all the rage of late, and that as you ponder *Unplugged* you may be asking yourself, "Do I *really* need another book on this?" To that I can only shake my head and bemuse, "When was the last time you read something so essential and so fundamental that it was, seemingly contradictorily, also awe-inspiring and revelatory? That it so infused your work with meaning and purpose that it improved the outright quality of your life—both on and off the field?"

This is *not* a book on employee engagement; it is something much more. It is something so grounding that it is electrifying and so utilitarian that it is transformational. It is about understanding what happens to employees when they lose their way amidst change, when they become unplugged from purpose, connection, direction, meaning, value, place. When they become, in a word, unmoored.

There is something to be said for moorings, for staying power, and for the ability to remain fresh, novel, and relevant whilst also remaining *true* in this era of flimflam, immediate gratification, fly-by-night TED talkers, social media darlings, and even more to be said for those whose contributions not only tilled a field but, in many ways, actually *discovered and defined* it. It is upon such shoulders that household names like James

Kouzes, Barry Posner, Marcus Buckingham, Susan Cain, Chip and Dan Heath, Lois Frankel, Adam Grant, Brené Brown, Simon Sinek, and Malcolm Gladwell have built their sparkly, effervescent brands.

Three decades before that ilk, Tom and Steve's sleeves were rolled up and their brows were dripping with sweat as they did the preliminary spade-work in organization after organization, company after company, team after team, both figuratively and literally proving Kurt Lewin's pro-verbial maxim, "There is nothing so practical as a good theory."

It was the case in 1987, the case the decade after that, the case in every collaboration and corporate interaction I've had the privilege to watch them work firsthand, and it will be the case forevermore because their work is built on *truth,* and truth—my friends—is *timeless.*

Truth cares not *one* iota for the ephemerality of politics, or fashion, or seasonality. It is not fickle or fair-weather; it is, on the contrary, as certain as North. It is undeniable, irrefutable, and indefatigable, whatever the eyeballs or technology we use at the time to find it.

Good work, built on truth, stands the test of time, and human energy and meaning are as essential today as they were at the dawn of humankind.

Rest assured in the incontrovertible: *Employee energy*—like positive attitude—*is a force multiplier.* In my own work at the intersections of strategy, inclusion, and postmodern management, I find again and again that the combination of *intrapersonal capabilities* (self, time, and emo-tion-management among them), *interpersonal skills,* and *the undergirding pillars of one's own attitude and energy* is the most reliable predictor of employee and organizational performance. Other things being equal, I'd put my money on anyone with the better attitude bout after bout and come up a winner no less than eighty percent of the time.

I am reminded of this when I ponder concentration camp survivor/ eventual logo-therapist Viktor Frankl's most poignant line in *Man's Search for Meaning:* "Everything can be taken from a man but one thing, the last of the human freedoms: To choose one's attitude in any given set of circumstances—to choose one's own way."

Choose energy and engagement as described herein and I promise buoyancy—the sort that will see you through storm to shore—because together they form the twin tides that reliably raise all boats.

May you be restored and renewed in the reading of it, and never lost again.

Blake Leath, PhD
Toronto, Ontario
May 22, 2018

Preface

As corporate officers, as researchers, and as authors, we first witnessed a trend that began with a focus on "downsizing" and its impact on employees in the early nineteen-eighties. The word was used to describe the permanent elimination of part of an organization's work force. Today this trend is most often referred to as a "reduction in force" (RIF) initiative. Downsizing was followed by an emphasis on "change management," a set of steps that transition an organization to a future state, first written about by Julien Phillips, a McKinsey consultant, in the journal Human Resource Management in 1982, though it was not extensively applied until ten years later.

Both of these trends were studied from the perspective of what can happen to the "energy" of an organization due to the trauma associated with change. Steve, with Harry Woodward, wrote the book *Aftershock: Helping People through Corporate Change* to address the aftermath of change and its influence on employees. In that book, one of the ways employees experienced change was "loss." It was noted that when employees experienced change with a feeling of loss, those employees became disengaged.

It is important to note, this was also the timeframe in which employees were losing their jobs – maybe for the first time, for reasons besides their own personal performance. This phenomenon had a major impact on breaking the bonds of loyalty between an organization and its employees. Performing at a high level was no longer security against being laid off. Employees believed companies were no longer loyal to them, so they questioned why they should be loyal to companies.

We witnessed the emergence of "engagement" in 1990 when William Kahn provided the first formal definition: "the harnessing of organization members' selves to their work roles." We, at that time, began to conduct research with various client companies focused on how to restore employee energy that was lost because of change. Restoring employees' energy enables them to become engaged once again.

The more we learned, the more we began to conclude that engagement is not really understood. Steve was present at a senior leadership meeting with one of his clients when a person from a consulting company provided an overview of engagement scores that the organization had received related to a series of categories such as communication, teaming, regard for their leader, support, recognition, development, etc. The scores were positive, and the leadership seemed satisfied that engagement was being properly addressed. A question was directed toward the consultant: "What is your definition of engagement?" His response was interesting. "When the scores you receive on the audit are high." Does this define engagement? It does if you accept a definition that bridges the pre-existing concept of "job satisfaction" and employee engagement, as Schmidt et al., (Journal of Applied Psychology, 2002) proposed: "an employee's involvement with, commitment to, and satisfaction with work."

We don't accept this definition. While we strongly believe there is a correlation between one's level of work satisfaction and one's level of engagement, we were still left with the questions, "What does engagement look like?" "How do we know the organization has it?"

Ask a group of managers or employees in a room to define what engagement is and what engagement looks like. You will hear them use descriptors such as "enthusiasm," "going the extra mile," "being happy," "putting in a full day's work," "involvement," and "having a positive attitude." Ask then to define what low engagement looks like, and the opposite is described: "lack of enthusiasm," "unhappy people," "lacking a work ethic," "lack of involvement," "having a negative attitude," etc. Do these define whether the employees of an organization are engaged or not? If you ask the same group of people to describe high morale and then low morale, you likely will hear similar words. While we agree these examples describe possible "attributes," the notion these attributes define engagement remain problematic.

Our endeavor in writing this book was to provide clear answers to a series of important questions:

- What is engagement?

- If employees are asked what they want/need to fully engaged, what are their responses?

- What are the primary reasons employees become disengaged?

- What cultural elements influence the level of engagement?

- What is the role of leadership in creating high engagement?

- What are the practices that can lead to a culture of engagement?

The content for this book is based on a combined sixty-plus years of working with organizations in the areas of leadership, change management, and communications. Extensive research was conducted by polling employees in both small and large corporations regarding engagement. To this we add the insights of numerous colleagues, business leaders, authors, and scholars who in so many ways have advanced our knowledge related to engagement. Also of importance, we have both been part of corporate America, having had in the past or currently having responsibility for how an organization performs and responsibility to a significant number of people who called us their leaders. What we present is not theory. It is a sharing of our real organizational experience related to employee engagement and a series of applications or specific ways to build a culture of engagement.

This book is written for leaders at all levels of the organization. We use the word "leader" rather than "manager" because we believe creating a culture of high engagement is a leader-led endeavor, regardless of a leader's specific level or title.

We invite readers to use this book as a guide for creating high engagement. Throughout the book, we will highlight critical insights. We will ask thought-provoking questions that allow the reader to relate the content to their own situation.

Engagement will be explored from two primary perspectives:

- Change and its influence on engagement. This explores the issue of choice and the elements that influence an employee's decision to engage in the change process.

- How to create a culture of engagement. This looks at how to create a set of leadership practices that create a culture of engagement.

In Chapter 1, readers are provided an example of how an organization disengages or, in essence, loses its spirit. Lessons the example teaches and the insights that were learned are provided. Engagement is defined, and the various choices employees make regarding engagement are outlined. Research findings regarding what employees want from leadership to be fully engaged are discussed, and finally, the five elements that make up a culture of engagement are introduced. They are:

- Perceived Opportunity
- Personal Accountability
- Inclusion
- Connectedness
- Validation

In Chapter 2, the role leadership plays in creating a culture of engagement is addressed. The cultural aspects of engagement are defined.

In Chapter 3, the first element of engagement, perceived opportunity, is discussed. The focus is on how to achieve employee buy-in to the organization's potential. A series of leadership interventions focused on realistic optimism will be introduced.

In Chapter 4, the second element of engagement will be explored: personal accountability. The focus is on how to help employees accept personal accountability for both their performance and their behavior.

In Chapter 5, the focus is on the third element of engagement, inclusion. The focus is on how to involve employees, inform employees, and encourage high communication.

In Chapter 6, the fourth element of engagement, connectedness, is introduced. The focus is on how to connect the right people to each other and work in a supportive team environment.

In Chapter 7, the fifth element of engagement, validation, addresses various ways to demonstrate interest in employees. Applications regarding how you support, develop, and recognize individuals are introduced.

In Chapter 8, a process to instill the five elements as part of the organization's culture is provided. Through a series of activities, an organization's leadership can establish how they introduce the elements of engagement into their culture.

The book is organized to provide leaders a way to think about the business context they are a part of. Elements that most influence engagement will be introduced, examples of best practices are provided, and readers will have the opportunity to address the business environment they are a part of and make choices about what is needed for their particular situation. An outcome will be to have an engagement strategy specific to the needs of the reader's organization. The reader should be able to answer the question, "What will lead our organization to a culture of engagement?"

Enjoy the journey.
Steve Buchholz
Tom Roth

Authors' Acknowledgments

This book began with a question: What takes the human energy out of an organization and how to get it back? Our journey to write this book began several years ago following the publication of *Aftershock: Helping People through Corporate Change* by Harry Woodward and Steve Buchholz. The book opened many doors with organizations going through various change events, and we wanted our participation in understanding what they experienced. Through the many years we worked with clients, we interviewed, surveyed, and partnered with a variety of organizations that worked with us to understand how organizations lose their energy and how to get it back. We want to especially thank the following individuals who took particular interest in our work and who contributed in a variety of ways to this book.

Dr. Buzz Cue, Dr. Jeff Ives, Dr. Mike Ganey, Dr. Karen Ferrante, Dr. Mary Sommers, Dr. Nancy Hutson and Arthur Hubbs, who led various research functions within Pfizer World Research and Development, Kathy Doyle, VP Human Resources, Foster Miller, Alan Perry, Sears, Jerry Schmidt, Caterpillar, Jane Agar, Michael Moss, Morgan Stanley Bank, Henry Griffith, IBM UK, William Flemming, Ross Vroman, John Benson, Fred

Haimes, Skanska US Building, Dave Olsen, healthcare consultant, and Rod Ambrosie, Wenck Associates.

We especially want to thank all of those who read this book in various drafts and gave us the benefit of their critique and wisdom:

Dr. Sarah Kelly, head of Pharmaceutical Sciences Small Molecule, Pfizer Worldwide Research and Development

Andy Fulton, President, MEGlobal

Dr. Alberto, Perez La Rotta, President, Wilson Learning Latin America

Joe Grabowski, CEO, Wenck Associates

Blake Leath, President, The Leath Group

Scott McLeod, COO, Skanska USA Building

Dr. Steve Ruggieri, COO, Foster-Miller/Qinetiq North America

Dr. Laura Campos, Siestra

We have also been enriched by the wisdom of those who most influenced our life journey: Larry Wilson, David Bradford, Alan Cohen, Harry Woodward, BC Husselton, Richard Leider, and George Land.

Finally, we wish to express our deep appreciation to the many leaders working within organizations who have been strong examples of essence-based leadership, rebuilding the spirit in their workplace.

Steve Buchholz
Tom Roth

Chapter 1

Unplugged—How an Organization's Employees Lose Their Energy

We're in the Energy Business

"What business are you in?" For years, one of the biggest challenges we've experienced has been explaining to others what we do for a living. Our formal response has been, "We research and design learning systems for organizations." To most people, this description doesn't mean much. As we try to further explain our business, the other person often concludes something like, "Oh, you're in the motivational business." At that point, we know we've failed miserably.

Several years ago, Steve was on a plane to Calgary, Alberta. The gentleman sitting next to him asked him what he did for a living. Steve tried to explain, but realized the man was just being polite when he said, "I understand." To reciprocate, Steve asked him what he did. The man replied he worked for a gas production company in Calgary, saying simply, "I'm in the energy business." As Steve recalls, a light bulb went off, and he realized he also was in the energy business. This began our journey to understand how energy is used during periods of significant organizational change. Now, when someone asks what business we're in, our reply is simple: "We're in the energy business—the human energy business." As is every manager or leader in any organization.

Employees are limited energy resources, and how they use their energy over the course of an eight-to-ten-hour day will determine the level of performance achieved, as indicated by engagement research. Leadership can mandate the amount of time an employee works, but it can't mandate the amount of *discretionary energy* (the energy over and above what is routinely needed to do one's job) invested by the employee.

> *Energy*, not time, is the fundamental currency of engagement.

This led us to increase our focus on understanding the ramifications of a disengaged work culture and what employees believed they needed to reengage. Our findings make up the core of this book.

In this chapter, we'll define engagement, identify what causes an organization to lose its energy or to disengage, discuss the role leadership plays in influencing choice, and present the key elements that lead to reengagement.

Engagement: You Will Know It When You See It

One of the questions we often ask in our consulting and training practice is, "What does engagement look like?" Everyone is able to describe what it looks like in the workplace—being high energy, having a take-charge attitude, participating at high levels, arriving early to work and staying late, and being committed and motivated. We then ask a second question, "How do you define engagement?" In response, after a long pause, we hear the same words used to describe what engagement looks like: "high energy, take-charge attitude, high levels of participation." Engagement is often simply described as the level of enthusiasm and dedication a worker feels toward his or her job. It's also described as the willingness to invest discretionary effort at work in order to go above and beyond what is expected.

The dictionary definition of engagement is vague and unclear, so one of the first things we wanted to do was to articulate clearly our definition of engagement.

Engagement Defined

Most people understand how powerful individuals' perceptions are related to the events happening around them and to them. Perception takes on even more significance in times of change because it consciously or unconsciously impacts the level of energy that employees will expend in response to the changes.

We define engagement as the combination of:

- The perception of the desired changes
- The amount of physical energy expended on the changes

Perception

Assume an organization has implemented a new initiative to increase project management efficiency. Every employee is expected to transition from the current project management system to the new one by the end of the month. What comes into play? The answer is perception. Employees may view the new project management system as either positive or negative. Or, maybe at this point, they're unable to decide. Perception can be represented on a continuum from negative to neutral to positive:

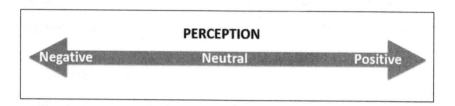

In this example, a negative perception implies the employees don't like the proposed project management system or they feel the current one works just fine and don't want any disruption caused by installing a new system. A neutral perception implies the employees are unsure or don't have enough information to determine if the planned implementation is good or bad, deciding to wait and see. If employees perceive the project management system as positive, they're saying positive things about the change, appearing excited about its prospects.

> For every change, every employee will decide if the change is positive, negative, or neutral

Energy

Similar to perception, you can represent expended energy on a continuum, from low to medium to high.

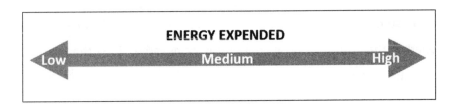

For every change, employees decide how much discretionary energy or effort they're going to expend responding to the change. Continuing with the project management example in terms of energy expenditure, several scenarios could occur. Employees could perceive the project management system as negative: They're losing a familiar process that seems to work just fine. Or, perhaps they don't see the purpose in changing at the moment. In both of these cases, employees would likely choose to invest minimal energy. Employees could also perceive the project management system as a positive addition to the organization, choosing, therefore, to commit a high level of energy. In yet another scenario, employees are uncertain and have more questions than answers, so they chose to limit their energy until a positive or negative conclusion is clearer.

Another situation is still possible. Employees may perceive the project management system as negative, but they choose to expend energy fighting the implementation they view as an unnecessary burden and expense—negative perception, but high energy. They may have high energy, but they spend it resisting change, not helping to execute the change.

> For every change or request asked of someone, that person will decide how much discretionary energy to invest.

In summary, when employees are asked to engage, they determine whether the request is positive, neutral, or negative. They then choose how much energy they will invest.

How employees demonstrate engagement

Engagement most clearly happens when employees decide to have a positive perception of what is happening in the organization, particularly in times of change, and then they choose to devote a high level of energy to executing the change and helping the organization drive its strategy and achieve its goals.

> Engagement: positive perception, high discretionary energy

This book focuses primarily on how high engagement organizations can become disengaged, or lose energy.

Disengagement: What Causes an Organization to Become Unplugged?

This true example illustrates how change can impact the human spirit and lead to disengagement in an organization we call Avcor Technologies. Perhaps you can relate to this story.

Avcor Technologies (Avcor) was a company where innovative practices led to exciting products. Employees referred to the company's culture as a creative greenhouse. The company leadership emphasized creating the next generation of smart products. Employees had many opportunities to explore emerging trends in a variety of settings and translate the lessons learned into a variety of applications.

The company leader, whom we refer to as Nancy, was described as visionary. She was a magnet for talented people who shared her vision for the future. She was gifted in her ability to bring out the best thinking in those she led. In fact, Avcor never conducted formal talent recruitment. If the company needed a new employee, Avcor asked current employees to reach out to their network of colleagues, and the candidates contacted Avcor. Nancy energized her employees, who worked together to build exciting products that were highly regarded in the marketplace. She placed a high premium on learning and believed strongly in giving employees the opportunity to grow in their roles.

The employees' commitment, energy, and sense of purpose were reflected in the quality of the products. The employees also shared a belief that the organization was doing something important for the world. This belief was reflected in the relationships they developed with their customers. Their strong customer base viewed themselves as an extension of Avcor. These customers participated in the company's customer forum to provide feedback on the latest ideas, developments, and products. They also referred their most trusted colleagues and friends to Avcor. The organization was at the top of its game. Employees were fully engaged.

Then, it all changed.

The trigger event was the announcement that a Fortune 500 company looking for an entrance into the markets served by Avcor had acquired the organization. Employees were told that partnership would bring many benefits: enhanced growth; additional product investment due to the size and financial strength of the acquiring company; and global market positioning (which Avcor had coveted, but hadn't been able to achieve on its own). The initial response by Avcor employees was mixed. Some employees received the news as positive, while others chose to wait and see.

For a while, Avcor remained basically the same organization, with little change in day-to-day operations. However, the first blow came when the parent company announced Nancy would be leaving the organization. Although it was suggested she left on her own, everyone knew she was bought out as part of the acquisition and had fulfilled her commitment to stay on during the transition period. After the acquisition, her level of energy also showed she wasn't happy with how the process was unfolding. Consequently, Avcor employees began to question the truthfulness of what they were being told, which led to an erosion of trust with the parent company.

A short time later, the parent company brought in one of its own vice presidents to run Avcor who had little experience running an innovative technology company. Although his intentions were positive, he didn't understand the business model, and more importantly, Avcor's corporate culture. Avcor, like many organizations focused on innovation and product development, didn't have a strong discipline around spending. The new leader brought a heavy focus on the financial expectations of the parent company with less attention on nurturing Avcor's experimental and creative culture.

What ensued was the unintentional dismantling of Avcor Technologies as a vibrant organization and a preferred place to work. Rather than increasing growth funding as had been expected, the parent company cut investments, restructured parts of the organization for efficiency, and let talented people go, all in an effort to make Avcor appear more profitable. This was the first time the organization had experienced layoffs. This downturn was made even bitterer by the fact that people were cut for reasons other their own personal performance. Over a short period of time, many senior management employees, the ones charged with implementing the layoffs they didn't agree with, saw investments dwindling and began to leave. In less than a year, Avcor's positive energy and engagement were lost. Avcor Technologies unplugged. Employees felt like the lights went out.

The remaining leaders gave it their best effort. Reengagement of the organization became a high priority, but lacked the know-how. Despite all the changes that the organization had been through, leadership decided to introduce even more changes. Leaders attempted to restructure, revise the strategy, introduce efficiency-based processes, bring in new talent, and revamp incentive systems. Instead of focusing on executing the strategy going forward, many employees questioned whether the changes would do any good and wondered when and what the next change would be. Eventually, people got burned out or put their energy on hold. The energy and passion that were once present became lost.

This situation raises a series of questions: What happened? What could the parent company have done differently to maintain the

9

innovative spirit? What did the employees personally experience that led to disengagement? What are the key practices that organizations can employ when moving through change to maintain or even increase employee engagement?

Although having different stories from Avcor Technologies, many organizations that have asked us these questions shared a similar outcome: disengagement.

Have you ever gone through a similar experience that resulted in disengagement of your organization? How did it feel? How did you react? How did your colleagues react?

What Are the Lessons You Can Learn from Avcor Technologies?

What is amazing to us is how many organizations have gone through, or are going through what Avcor experienced. It's important to understand and learn from those experiences, so you can more effectively deal with if and when it happens to you.

Lesson one: the role "perceived loss" plays

The fundamental premise of how change affects an organization is simple: If employees perceive change as primarily a *gain* (positive for the organization and for them personally), the process of moving through change essentially isn't an issue. Even though the complexity of the change may create challenges, employees stay engaged. On the other hand, if the majority of employees perceive the change as a loss, disengagement is likely, with employees becoming stuck in the change rather than moving through it. Dealing with the complexities and adapting to the changes become far more difficult.

> The perception of gain gives employees energy; the perception of loss takes it away.

When an organization is going through change, employees try to understand the implications for both the organization and for themselves personally. At the organizational level, they're processing how the changes impact their department's priorities, projects, and budgets, along with how the changes will impact the organization's ability to succeed.

On a personal level, employees also evaluate how the changes will affect them. When employees perceive the changes as positive and personally beneficial to them, they become your biggest advocates and supporters. They'll invest their energy to ensure they're doing everything possible to make the changes successful. Why? Because employees believe there is a personal benefit in doing so. When employees perceive the changes will result in a loss to them personally, even if the changes benefit the organization, their energy levels will drop.

Furthermore, understand that people react to change both intellectually and emotionally. Intellectually, they may understand the importance and appropriateness of the changes and how the changes will help drive the organization's strategy and success in the marketplace. Emotionally, however, if they personally experience more loss than gain, some employees find it difficult to find the energy needed to execute the changes. We believe, in most situations, "emotional" overrides "intellectual" when employees are choosing how to invest their energy.

In these situations, where upper management sees the changes as a gain and employees see the changes as a loss, employees are often labeled as "resisting change." Our experience tells us they may not be resisting change, but, instead, they lack the readiness to engage. Employees haven't come to grips with their own sense of loss, and no one in the organization is helping them do so. Leaders must understand and address the emotional impact of change on employees before they can reinforce the intellectual benefits to the change; otherwise, employees may not be ready to move on and execute the changes with high energy.

At Avcor Technologies, employees were "living in the loss." They were, in a sense, grieving for what was. Living in the loss leaves little energy left for work. Instead, much of their energy went into taking care of themselves and each other.

Return to the Avcor Technologies case. What are the various ways these employees experienced loss?

The experience of loss

Most leaders focus on the big picture of why the organization needs to change and have a clear vision of the desired outcomes of the change. Because employees haven't been part of the change discussion, they lack the intellectual clarity that leaders have. Leaders need to lower their line of sight and try to understand how employees are experiencing the changes, which quite often is with a sense of loss.

How loss is expressed

Loss can be experienced in a variety of ways. Here are some examples:

Type of loss	What employees may be thinking or saying
Relationships	"Many of my colleagues and friends are gone."
Identity	"I used to be known for my. . ."
Structure: • Physical • Functional	"I lost my office with a window." "We're being asked to do different things. . ."
Future	"I used to feel my job was safe."
Meaning	"I can't understand why. . ."
Purpose	"I didn't sign up to do this."
Influence	"No one asks for my thoughts anymore."
Tradition	"We're not family-friendly anymore."
Stability	"I'm not sure what is going to happen next."
Entitlement	"I used to be able to count on a bonus."
Control	"I used to control my own destiny."
Hope	"I don't think we can survive."

Some of these losses may seem insignificant from a leadership point of view, but they're extremely important to the employees.

Conversely, each one of these situations can also be experienced in a different light if perceived as a gain. For example: "I gained an office with a window." "I now have a stronger sense of purpose." "Now, I feel more in control of my destination." "The new bonus system is much better than what we had." When employees view the changes as gains, the changes can give them energy.

> **The next time your company is about to experience change, ask yourself, "How are employees likely to experience gain or loss?"**

Lesson two: Loss comes "in code"

As we followed the Avcor story, we observed how difficult it was for the company to restore energy with so many employees living in the loss. This led us to explore how loss can be experienced or exhibited. We discovered four basic patterns: disorientation, discontent, disidentification, and disengagement. We decided to label so that both employees and leaders can recognize what is happening and, therefore, begin to do something about it.

Disorientation

For some employees, loss creates disorientation. *Disorientation* occurs when an employee is confused or unclear about what is happening. Typically, the employee has many more questions than answers. The employee feels his or her current situation is up in the air, chaotic, unreal, unclear, empty, or confusing. Struggling with how to move forward, the employee fails to commit to the new reality. The employee isn't necessarily experiencing loss, but, rather, he or she feels lost.

Dave Noer in his book, *Healing the Wounds: Overcoming the Trauma of Layoffs and Revitalizing Downsized Organizations*, captured part of this when he stated, "Employees are desperately seeking assurance that the cafeteria will be operating, the paychecks will not bounce, the softball league will continue, the Monday morning staff meetings will take place." On one hand, these issues may seem trivial within the larger scheme of things. However, when someone is feeling lost and disoriented, trying to hold on to even the simplest of things can seem like a big deal. As change disrupts the employees' work environment, they want to know how they will fit in and seek to understand what the new normal will be.

For example, Nick stops by his manager's office at least once a day, asking questions to seek assurance that he is a part of the organization's future. He often seems confused about what is expected of him and appears worried. His role and responsibilities have been explained to him in terms of the what but likely not the how and the why, so he continues to wonder out loud: "What is going on?" "When will we know something?" "Is everyone as confused as I am?" He spends a lot of time preparing for work, but never seems to get around to getting started. His energy is focused on feeling safe and included.

Discontent

Some employees experience loss as discontent. *Discontent* occurs when an employee is angry or frustrated with the changes that have occurred or with the leadership that initiated them. An employee comes across as being critical and talks negatively about the changes, attacking the people in charge who made the changes. Underneath this discontent is a feeling that the changes are bad for the organization and/or for the employee.

Employees who are experiencing discontent are often vocal with their opinions and don't seem to mind who knows it. These employees can easily bring down their colleagues' energy levels. By hearing how negative things are, their colleagues may wonder whether they should be upset too because discontent often drains energy from others.

15

For example, Beth can be unpredictable these days. She roared into her manager's office this morning and launched into a tirade about everything that's wrong with the changes. This is unusual, because Beth is described as a high performer who solves problems rather than raising them. "Maybe I should quit," she said as she left. She's obviously frustrated by the changes. Last week in a meeting, she spent about fifteen minutes explaining how senior management doesn't have a clue. By the time she was finished, half the people in the room were angry as well. Beth has always been one of the most influential leaders in the organization. When she gets angry, other people do, too.

Disidentification

Some employees experience loss as disidentification. *Disidentification* occurs when an employee focuses more on what was rather than on what will be. The individual identifies strongly with the past and with what no longer exists. The telling phrase is often, "I used to. . .and now I. . ."; for example, "I used to have a lot of say in this organization, and now I'm outside of the circle of influence." This employee spends a lot of time complaining about present circumstances or trying to convince others that the past was better than the future. The motivation for complaining is an underlying belief that, "If enough of us complain, maybe we'll go back to the way things were." Moving toward the new reality is hindered because the employee doesn't want to let go of the past.

For example, Bob isn't engaged in his current work. He spends his discretionary time telling others how much better things used to be before the changes. In meetings, he focuses on what isn't working, rather than on what is working. He tends to discount any new ideas by talking about how the current processes are doing the job. Frequently, he's heard saying, "Why did we have to change anyway? It was working just fine." He continues to believe the organization will wake up to the fact that what used to be is better than what exists now.

Disengagement

Some employees experience loss through disengagement. *Disengagement* occurs when an employee invests little or no discretionary energy. The employee may withdraw, pull back, wait and see, or become quiet. He or she may appear to be involved and uses phrases like "no problem" or "everything is fine," but using these phrases often hides the true feelings that prevent commitment to the new reality. The employee will continue to put in time but will invest little energy. Disengagement correlates directly to perceived loss. The greater the loss, the greater the likelihood of disengagement.

For example, Clare has always been involved in everything and is eager to help. But now, she just sits back in her chair, remaining quiet and uninvolved. She used to be friendly and gregarious with a kind word for anyone who happened by. Now, her door is closed most of the time, and she doesn't seem to be accessible. She tells management what they want to hear, not what they need to hear. Her energy has disappeared. Yet, when asks how she's doing, she'll say, "Okay." It's obvious to her colleagues, though, that it isn't.

The greater the perceived loss, the greater the likelihood of disengagement.

17

Based on a questionnaire we gave to more than 5,000 employees from various organizations, research revealed disengagement was by far the most common way employees reacted to perceived loss. The first three patterns of loss (disorientation, discontent, and disidentification) can certainly cause employees to stay stuck in change, but they don't necessarily result in energy loss. Disengagement, on the other hand, does. As stated earlier, learning that disengagement is the predominant way employees react to loss, we decided to increase our focus on understanding the ramifications of a disengaged work culture and what employees felt was needed for reengagement.

In summary, loss comes in code. The symptoms of loss are played out through employees who appear disoriented, discontent, disidentified, and disengaged. Leaders who recognize these patterns will be able to better support employees who are living in the loss, reengage them, and help them move forward with energy. Without this insight, leaders will simply describe these employees as experiencing "low morale." This general, low-morale label does a real disservice to their employees and disregards what they're experiencing.

Recognize how employees are demonstrating loss

If leaders can recognize the four general ways loss is demonstrated, then the antidote to these behaviors is often fairly straightforward.

If loss is demonstrated by:	Leaders need to:
Disorientation	Reorient by clarifying direction, providing clear expectations and goals, and defining roles.
Discontent	Understand the reason for the anger (usually a form of loss), listen while the employees vent, focus on the cause, and try to move them through it.
Disidentification	Help the employee identify with the future by creating a sense of opportunity in what is coming.
Disengagement	Help the employee reengage by developing the five elements of engagement (featured later as chapters of this book).

In our current roles, we have had the opportunity to work with a variety of organizations, helping them understand the impact of disruptive change. Although our work helps leaders understand what can occur when loss is experienced, the larger issue is how to restore the energy of organizations whose employees have become disengaged. To accomplish this, organizations need to focus on the key elements that restore energy and reengage an organization, discussed later in the book. Yes, you can turn the lights back on.

Lesson three: Repetitive change leads to change fatigue

In his book, *Managing as a Performing Art: New Ideas for a World of Chaotic Change,* Peter Vaill introduces an intriguing metaphor for the change, uncertainty, and turbulence that now characterize organizational life: "permanent whitewater." His premise is change begets change, and organizations will need to adapt to this reality. In the Avcor Technologies case, leadership felt the solution to observing disengagement was to introduce yet more change. However, if an organization is frequently changing, it can result in a form of fatigue, leading to more chronic and ongoing disengagement.

The following model provides a visual of what can happen to employees who experience frequent change events.

The Energy Continuum

The Energy Continuum describes various ways energy disperses and becomes consequential to the organization's effectiveness.

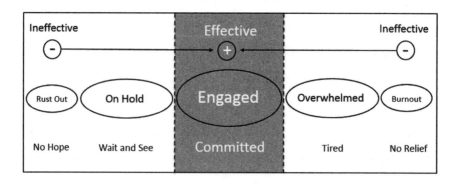

Remaining engaged

You want employees to be in the center of the model. Naturally, for a change initiative to be executed, the discretionary energy of the majority of the employees needs to engaged. When employees are engaged, effectiveness is at its peak and commitment is high. But during change events, especially prolonged or frequent change events, energy tends to disperse to the right or left of center and leads to ineffectiveness.

Becoming overwhelmed

From the center engaged part of the model, energy can flow to the right because frequent change can often lead to a feeling of being overwhelmed. In their book, *The Power of Full Engagement: Managing Energy, Not Time, is the Key to High Performance and Personal Renewal*, Jim Loehr and Tony Schwartz define being overwhelmed as "expending more energy than one is recovering." Feeling overwhelmed occurs for a variety of reasons: having a personal energy level below what is needed to meet performance demands; having too much to do, with too little time to do it; being given the responsibilities and workload of others who have left the organization; and conflicting demands. Often, employees feel they have lost control of their "self." They can no longer balance critical portions of their lives. The need to spend an inordinate amount of time meeting work demands takes precedent in their lives.

A lack of focus and sense of priority can also lead to feeling over-whelmed. Especially during major change, the organization may experience "initiative overload," which places much energy on starting new priorities. Hence, it's best to focus on the critical few priorities and do those well.

Feeling overwhelmed can be a condition that the organization's work culture finds itself in as well, which you can demonstrate by conducting a simple exercise with about eight people. Have participants form a circle. Introduce a soft ball and ask participants to pass the ball around the circle, with each person catching and throwing the ball once. Everyone has a designated person to whom they will throw the ball and another from whom they will receive the ball. The ball will move quickly around the circle without problems. Then, introduce a second ball and ask them to keep both balls moving around the circle. Even adding a third ball is still a manageable workload. However, as balls are continuously added to the circle, participants will reach a point where the system begins to over-whelm them. Balls are dropped, or the accuracy of the toss diminishes. When someone doesn't catch a ball and attempts to retrieve it, other balls don't stop being tossed, adding to the number of misplayed balls. Eventually, the game collapses.

What happens in corporations? Work is productive when everyone has a manageable workload. Things run smoothly. But when more tasks are added and complexity increases, the system can become overwhelmed. Tasks are forgotten or not completed, quality decreases, mistakes are made, and relationship tension increases. If the conditions that led to feeling overwhelmed aren't corrected, employees can begin to experience occupational burnout.

Experiencing burnout

If there is no relief from being overwhelmed, an employee can move to experience burnout. *Burnout* describes an employee who is experiencing long-term exhaustion or unrecoverable fatigue. This results in diminished interest in or capability to carry out work—a form of disengagement. Christina Maslach and Susan Jackson, authors of the *Maslach Burnout Inventory*, operationalize burnout as a three-dimensional syndrome made of exhaustion, cynicism, and inefficacy. Fatigue is cited as one of the causes leading to burnout; as a result, the employee doesn't have energy for work and is described as running on empty. Interestingly, Maslach and Jackson define the opposite of burnout as "engagement," characterized by energy, involvement, and efficacy.

Feeling burned out can lead an employee to put what energy he or she has on hold—one of the processes of disengagement.

Putting energy on hold

Again from the center engaged part of the model, the flow of energy can move to the left when employees put their energy on hold. When employees put energy on hold, they disengage. Disengaged employees invest little discretionary energy to their work. They put in their time but not their positive energy. The primary trigger to put energy on hold is the perception of loss. The second-most frequent reason is change fatigue.

An organization announcing another round of pending changes is often accompanied by employees putting their energy on hold. Buzz Cue, formerly Pfizer's site head focused on pharmaceutical sciences, described the numerous rounds of change as a "pathology of endlessness." In these situations, employees question whether they have the energy needed to go through yet more change. A form of learned apathy also sets in over time. Employees begin to question why they should give their energy, believing, "It's all going to change again anyway." If employees stay in a holding pattern for a significant amount of time, the behavior can lead to rust-out, the death of ambition.

Experiencing rust-out

Rust-out occurs when employees psychologically unplug from the organization: They can't wait until the end of the working day, and they count the days to retirement. They use what energy they do have to remain undiscovered. Reengaging individuals at this point on the continuum becomes extremely challenging.

> Employees who are experiencing the death of ambition use their energy to remain undiscovered.

In sessions with leaders on change management, we often asked, "Where on the continuum would you place most employees in your organization?" The answers varied from "all over the continuum" to "it depends." Leaders then shared that certain departments were harder hit or that change affected only a certain part of their organization. As a result, some employees were engaged while others were either overwhelmed or had put their energy on hold.

With many, their answers expressed that they were overwhelmed:

- "Our people have so much to do."
- "We have half the staff we used to and the burden to do the work has been placed on those who still have a job."
- "I have to work a ten-hour day just to keep up with the demands."

Unfortunately, these examples show how work satisfaction diminishes, resulting in employees with even less energy to keep up the pace.

Most companies didn't respond with the answer, "on hold," until they thought more deeply about their situation. They concluded it was easier to talk about being overwhelmed than talking about having no energy for work. In other words, many employees wanted to let their leaders know that they were putting in long hours or juggling many demands. For some, being overwhelmed was a badge of honor. On the other hand, those on the left half of the model felt they couldn't talk to management about not having energy for work because of unforeseen, potential consequences. They even gave the appearance of working hard rather than talking about why they had lost their energy.

Our research indicates the vast majority of employees going through frequent change put their energy on hold, and a startling number (about twelve percent) readily admit they lost their ambition and felt they were rusting out.

Where are your employees on the energy continuum?

Lesson four: How much energy employees give at work is their choice

When an organization is required to change in response to external and internal demands, everyone in the organization makes a choice, consciously or unconsciously, about how they'll use their energy. Whether a simple request is made of an employee ("Will you be part of a limited-duration team, focusing on improving cross-selling?") or a major change

25

initiative is implemented ("We are announcing a new organizational initiative to improve processes"), the employee makes an energy choice.

The Choice Model illustrates a variety of scenarios for how employees choose to use their energy.

The Choice Model

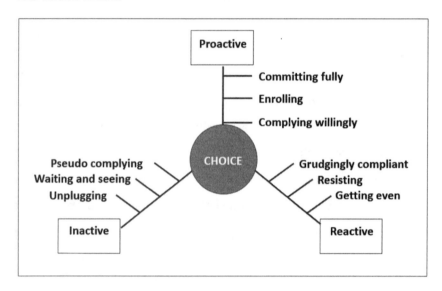

Every time you make a request, large or small, your employees make one of these choices.

Individuals have three primary categories of choices to make when deciding how to use their energy: proactive, reactive, or inactive. Within these broad categories, there are differences based on the three levels of perception (negative, neutral, and positive) and the three levels of energy expended (low, medium, and high).

Proactive

When employees chose to expend energy in a positive way, they're described as *proactive*. The varying degrees of expended energy are:

- **Complying willingly:** *Complying willingly* is a demonstration of being moderately positive, but expending a low level of energy: "I'll go along with it." Leaders often mistake willful compliance as having everyone on board and supportive of the changes. They're later surprised that little is being done to implement the required changes.

- **Enrolling:** *Enrolling* occurs when employees exhibit moderate levels of energy in a positive way. The employee is engaged but not fully: "Sounds good, count me in."

- **Committing fully:** However, employees who are *committing fully* expend a high level of energy in a positive way in response to the challenges and needs of the organization: "How can I get involved?" This is an important part of our definition of engagement.

Reactive

Employees who chose to use their energy to oppose or argue against change are described as *reactive*. Again, the three varying degrees are:

- **Complying grudgingly:** *Complying grudgingly* is a demonstration of an employee negatively perceiving what is being requested but feeling compelled or coerced to invest some energy to minimize some risk: "I feel I have to do it or else I may lose my job."

- **Resisting:** *Resisting* change occurs when employees perceive change or requests as negative, and they choose to put energy into fighting the changes or convincing other employees that it's a bad idea or strategy: "I don't agree, and I'm going to fight this decision."

- **Getting even:** *Getting even* can happen when employees experience change through a sense of personal or damaging loss. Employees are motivated to use their energy to get even, which can take the form of badmouthing leadership, theft, legal recourse, or sabotage: "I'm going to tell customers how the organization cut corners on quality."

Inactive

The choice to be inactive is a form of disengagement that occurs when employees choose to withhold their energy, to be in a period of waiting, or to withdraw. The three degrees of inactive choices, which are all forms of disengagement, are:

- **Pseudo complying:** *Pseudo complying* is when employees give the impression that they are positive and expending some energy, when in reality they aren't: "Look at me, busy, busy, busy."

- **Waiting and seeing:** *Waiting and seeing* is demonstrated when employees choose to put their energy on hold. They are, in essence, sitting in the stands rather than playing on the field. Employees remain neutral and withhold their energy until they either better understand the situation in a positive way or are swayed to act in some manner: "I'll just wait and see, then decide."

- **Unplugging:** *Unplugging* happens when employees have quit and stayed or have made the decision to leave but have yet to do so. They're negative and have no energy for work. Their self-talk may be: "I can't wait until I am out of here."

> *After a major change, which choice do you believe the majority of employees make: Proactive? Reactive? Inactive?*

What Research Revealed

To understand change and engagement, we needed the employee perspective. To do so, we interviewed or polled more than 5,000 employees and managers from more than twenty large and small organizations who had recently experienced major organizational changes. The changes these companies experienced included downsizing, restructuring, leadership or key personnel change, processes or workflow change, and mergers or acquisitions. The purpose was to determine how energy was used after the changes were announced.

What We Learned

When we looked at all cases where the perception of loss was greater than the perception of gain or where change-fatigue had set in, the results of energy choices across the three categories were:

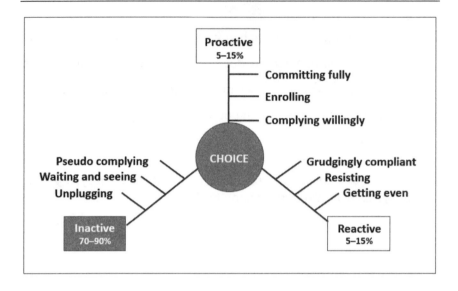

For example, a major company had gone through significant changes. Most of these changes were perceived as loss—loss of employees, loss of future opportunity, spending cuts, departure of well-regarded leaders, and site closings. An audit of these employees revealed eleven percent were proactive (mostly complying willingly), fourteen percent were reactive (mostly complying grudgingly), and seventy-five percent were inactive (mostly waiting and seeing).

The low percentage representing reactive was a surprise. Reactive behavior may appear higher in loss scenarios because reactive behavior can be visible. We also learned that although leadership often talks about employees resisting change, in some cases, this belief is a misperception. The issue isn't necessarily resistance; rather, it's more often a case of readiness.

We ascertained that during times of discontinuous change where loss is experienced and/or change fatigue is high, fully seventy to ninety percent of employees' experience one of the inactive levels—just doing their jobs, waiting and seeing, unwilling to expend energy lest the next change wipes out their efforts, using their energy to protect themselves, keeping their heads down, quitting but staying, or looking for new jobs.

If you're going through a major change initiative and seventy to ninety percent of your employees are keeping their heads down or have quit and stayed, how do you like your chances to execute your changes?

> Leaders often describe employees as resisting change, when in reality the issue is usually a lack of readiness to change.

We also noted if leadership couldn't influence the energy in a positive way (moving employees toward proactivity), the organization would begin to experience *entropy,* a gradual increase in disengagement, negativity, and a decline in its ability to function in a sustainable manner.

Lesson five: Organizations can disengage in a short period of time, while reengaging is a longer, more difficult undertaking

What continues to amaze us is how fast change can affect the energy and engagement of people at work. It's indeed like unplugging a key source of energy. What does that feel and look like?

Employees at Avcor Technologies quickly became disengaged; the place became quiet and sullen. Work continued to get done, but the energy and enthusiasm that had characterized the work culture was put on hold as employees took a wait-and-see attitude. Over time, the majority of the once-positive and energized employees left, either on their own or were let go. Several attempts to restore the energy ensued, but with limited results. The energy was gone.

Certainly, not all organizations go through such a dramatic upheaval as Avcor, but the reality is most organizations today experience ongoing, discontinuous change, resulting in the same problem: disengaged employees.

What became clear at Avcor was that the remaining leaders became frustrated with the limited results of their efforts to restore energy and a positive work culture. Not knowing what to do next, they also lost some of their energy; acting positive and enthusiastic became difficult.

Although an organization can appear to disengage in a short period of time, we conclude reengagement is a longer, more difficult undertaking. For many organizations, the level of energy that once existed can never be restored.

Low Job Satisfaction Leads to Disengagement

We have been highlighting lessons learned from the Avcor experience, brought on by both dramatic and ongoing change. Although not directly related to Avcor, another important disengagement contributor warrants some discussion. Another reason for energy being put on hold is a low level of work satisfaction. Having energy for work is difficult when an employee doesn't like his or her job, has a poor relationship with the boss, or feels accomplishments aren't acknowledged.

Low work satisfaction can occur because of change or exist absent of change. *Job satisfaction* is the positive response an employee has to specific facets of his or her job or to his or her feelings about the job.

A variety of factors contribute to low work satisfaction and, consequently, disengagement, including when an employee:

- is in a routine job with no challenge;
- doesn't like what he or she is being asked to do;
- experiences continuous change;
- isn't playing to his or her strengths;
- isn't given the tools and skills to do his or her job;
- receives no recognition or reward for good or exceptional performance;
- perceives that coworkers' poor performance isn't addressed;
- doesn't feel involved;
- feels not listened to;
- believes he or she isn't being informed;
- perceives a lack of professional development;
- feels unsupported;
- thinks he or she works for a poor manager or leader;
- feels his or her boss is toxic (takes his or her energy); or
- believes his or her boss doesn't care.

The measurement of engagement has primarily focused on work satisfaction using a series of questions similar to what the Gallup organization uses. For example, "I feel I can approach my manager with any type of question." The assumption is low scores indicate lower engagement and high scores indicate high engagement.

Leadership typically responds to low engagement findings by specifically addressing the low scores. For example, an organization may receive a low score in the area of recognition, so it launches an initiative to increase recognition for a job well done, believing that it has addressed the issue of disengagement. The idea is if employees feel they are receiving more recognition, their engagement should increase.

That's all well and good. But as organizations have implemented a wide variety of engagement programs over the years, Gallup has reported little improvement in engagement scores. They continue to report that less than a third of Americans are engaged at work, a number that has remained consistent since 2000 (*Gallup Business Journal*, 2015, vol. XX). Other HR development studies also confirm low engagement truly remains a global issue.

Although not the focus of this book, knowing the job-satisfaction level of each of your employees is an essential aspect of organizational health.

Many engagement audits correlate high and low work satisfaction to corresponding levels of engagement.

Leadership's Role

One of the key aspects of a highly engaged work culture is having a leader, or even more powerful, leadership who understands what it means to give energy to the organization rather than take it away. Multiple publications (research, articles, and books) have articulated the decreasing percentage of employees who are fully engaged at work and conversely the increasing percentage of employees who are disengaged. This news isn't new; in fact, it's a continuing trend. Clearly, the research from several different resources establishes the importance of learning how to increase the level of engagement in organizations and doesn't need further discussion here.

Yet, important questions remain. If everyone understands the importance of improving employee engagement, what are organizations doing about it? When an engaged organization becomes unplugged and loses its energy, what is its reengagement strategy? Which companies will find a way to change the flow of energy from outward to inward? Which leaders will know how to engineer their culture to achieve higher engagement?

In order to identify the key strategies that leaders can use to influence reengagement, understand the choices that employees make during times of disruptive change. We'll introduce, from their perspective, what employees want from leadership in order to feel fully engaged. And, we'll introduce five sets of practices (elements) that have the most influence on an organization's journey of reengagement.

Leadership's role is to influence how change is perceived as well as the choices employees make about how they will use their energy.

> In essence, the role of leadership is to influence how employees perceive the impact of change on the organization and how they choose to use their energy.

Getting the Energy Back: Reengaging the Organization

Our research didn't simply focus on the choices that employees made regarding levels of engagement; its primary focus was on what employees reported they needed from their leadership in order to reengage or remain engaged. In our research, we asked a simple question:

During these periods of change, what do you believe you need from your leadership?

> **How do you believe your employees would respond to this question?**

Findings

Six general clusters of responses emerged from the research, providing a theme and clarification of what employees need from their leadership:

A sense of future opportunity	Employees want to understand what the future holds for them. They want to feel a sense of hope. What in the future can they get excited about? What about the future will benefit them? Without a sense of future opportunity to move toward, they'll live in the loss rather than move through it.
Clear focus and expectations	Employees want their questions answered: "As a result of the changes, what do you now expect of us?" "How will we be held accountable?" Losing focus or becoming disoriented during times of change is common. Employees want to know how the change will impact them and what leadership expects of them.

A desire to feel informed	Employees want to feel included. They want to participate in authoring the future. All aspects of communication come into play: increased communication, the chance to provide input, the opportunity to discuss issues and ask questions, and the chance to be heard and involved.
A need to feel part of the team	Employees want to feel connected to each other. They want to feel they're part of a collaborative environment where support for each other is present.
Demonstrated interest in them	Employees want leaders to care about them. They want to feel they're an important part of the organization's future and want to be supported, recognized, and developed.
Leaders' examples	Employees want leadership to set the example and to walk the talk. During times of change, employees want to see their leaders out front.

Key questions to ask

If you turn these responses into questions that employees ask themselves during periods of change, they would translate to the following:

- Why should we get excited about reengaging?
- How will we be held personally accountable?
- How will we provide input into what is happening and be informed about important issues?
- How will we work effectively with each other?

- How will we be supported?

- How is leadership going to show up?

We looked at these clusters of responses and questions and identified five elements that directly influence both of the dimensions of engagement (perception and energy expended). We strongly believe these elements influence the choices employees make, leading to high engagement. The following model illustrates the following book chapters:

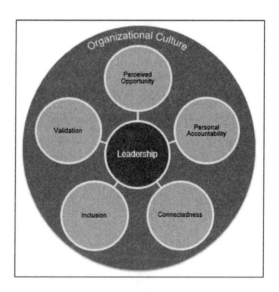

Chapter 2: Leadership's Example. There is a specific type of leadership—we call *essence-based leadership*—required to develop the five elements of engagement.

Chapter 3: The Element of Perceived Opportunity. Engagement happens when employees feel they're part of something important and have something to believe in.

Chapter 4: The Element of Personal Accountability. Engagement happens when employees are clear on what is expected of them and know why it's important to give their best. When this happens, personal accountability increases.

Chapter 5: The Element of Connectedness. Engagement happens when employees feel connected with each other, focus on mutual interest, and operate with shared responsibility. They create a collaborative mindset.

Chapter 6: The Element of Inclusion. Engagement happens when employees are well informed and involved and when they have an opportunity to openly express their thoughts and feelings. Simply stated, people want to feel "in" on things, including all aspects of the communication process.

Chapter 7: The Element of Validation. Engagement happens when employees feel that they matter and that they have a valued place in the organization. Three elements of validation include support, recognition, and reward.

Chapter 8: Creating a Culture of Engagement. You can use this guide to zero-in on areas of focus for an existing leadership team or each time a leader needs to assemble a team and address the engagement needs of the organization.

Chapter Summary

The currency of engagement is how discretionary energy is being invested. Organizational change often disperses energy. Employees, as a result of change, may experience a variety of energy-related responses— the overuse of their energy (feeling overwhelmed or burned out) or the underuse of their energy (disengaged or the death of ambition).

When employees are asked to change, they make the choice to be proactive, reactive, or inactive. When change is experienced as loss, or when employees are experiencing change fatigue, they often choose to disengage by becoming pseudo compliant, making the choice to wait and see, or unplugging. The role of leadership is to influence that choice. When the employee experiences change as positive and expends productive energy, engagement occurs.

The key responsibilities of leadership are to refocus the energy and reengage employees. To do so, leaders must understand, from the employees' perspective, what is needed for reengagement. These five elements are key to either maintaining engagement or recovering lost engagement:

1. Perceived opportunity
2. Personal accountability
3. Connectedness
4. Inclusion
5. Validation

The next chapter will look at the role leadership plays in reengagement, plugging back into the organization's energy supply—the performance of its employees.

Chapter 2

Leadership's Example

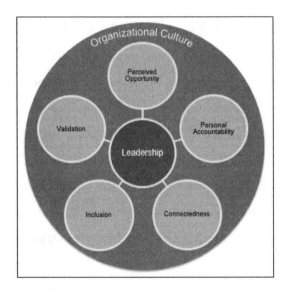

Premise: There is a specific type of leadership—we call *essence-based leadership*—required to exemplify and develop the five elements of engagement.

Whether disengagement has occurred because change has been experienced as a loss, continuous change has created fatigue, or employees feel a decline in job satisfaction, what role leadership plays in recognizing what occurred and how leadership appropriately responds are critical.

Think again about the Avcor Technologies example: It's amazing how one person in a position of authority can influence the direction of an organization. At the beginning, Avcor's visionary leader, Nancy, brought energy to the organization. She empowered employees, placed a high priority on learning, encouraged their development, motivated her employees, and cared deeply for people. When she left, employees felt a deep loss.

Her replacement took energy out of the organization. He brought a focus on efficiency, putting his energy in to cutting costs and cutting people rather than identifying ways the organization could be more effective. He limited the opportunities for employees to exercise their creative abilities in designing new software products. He was much more of a manager (doing things right) than he was a leader (doing the right things). His financial background oriented him to the numbers rather than to the people aspect of his role. His constituency wasn't the employees, but the stockholders. His goal was a stronger bottom line that satisfied the parent organization.

To address all of the challenges he faced, he introduced more changes intended to impact the organization's performance. What he failed to do was address the employees' loss of energy brought on by the changes and the overall change-fatigue. As a result, he lost his followership, who, in turn had lost their energy.

Understanding that leaders either give energy to the organization or take energy out of the organization is of utmost importance. Giving energy leads to engagement. Taking energy leads to disengagement.

Leaders often underestimate how much daily effort it takes to give the organization energy.

> Leaders either give energy or take energy out of the organization.

Creating a Leadership That Others Choose to Follow

> Ultimately you won't be judged so much by how well you lead, but how well you are followed

In chapter one, we introduced the idea that one of the key aspects of a highly engaged work culture is having a leader or even more powerful leadership that knows what it means to give energy to the organization rather than take energy out of the organization. If you believe this statement, then the obvious question is what kind of leadership inspires others to follow? That's the key question of this chapter. We will attempt to answer this question by first asking you to reflect on your own experience with effective leadership.

Reflecting on your "best leader"

When defining engagement earlier, we stated sometimes it's difficult to define what it is, but you'll know it when you see it. The same can be true for defining effective leadership. Throughout life, you've probably been in the presence of leaders who energized you and who inspired you to follow them. More than likely you've experienced them in a variety of settings, whether at work, in your family, or in your social friends, education, civic, political, religious, or athletic situations.

When working with the leadership of an organization, we often conduct a short two-part exercise. We first ask the simple question:

"Who is the person in your life you consider to be your best leader? (You decide what 'best leader' means to you.)"

When we think of leadership, we often do so in the context of managers in an organization, and people will say things like, "I had a boss who. . . ." Interestingly enough, when we ask people to identify their best leader, quite a few identify someone outside of work, for example, family members (parents), teachers, or coaches who inspired them.

The second part of the exercise is to reflect on the following questions:

"What is it about this person that caused you to pick him or her as your best leader? What were the qualities or characteristics this person exemplified?"

> *Before you read any further, take a few minutes to think about your best leader and write down the characteristics of this person that caused you to choose this person as your best leader.*

We have done this exercise for many years with a wide variety of audiences all around the world. We write the people's answers on a flip chart for all to see. It's amazing how similar the list of characteristics is regardless of group or location. Here is a representative sample of the kinds of words people use to describe their best leader:

Characteristics of a "Best Leader"

High Integrity	Provided good feedback
Honest	Believed in me
Set clear direction	Trusting
Caring	Humble
Courageous	Set challenging goals
Good listener	Fairness
Compassionate	Authentic
Self-confident	Respectful

If you look over the list, what do you notice about the words? The words *integrity, honest, caring, courageous, compassionate, self-confident, believed in me, trusting, humble, fairness, authentic, respectful* speak to the leader's character, or what a leader wants to *BE*. The remaining characteristics—*set clear direction, good active listener, provided good feedback,* and *set challenging goals*—speak to what a leader needs to *DO*. Without fail, every time we do this exercise, we always get a much higher percentage of character-based words included in the list, similar to what you see represented.

The essence and form of leadership

Character-based, or what we refer to as *essence-based* leadership, speaks to one's being and represents those core qualities driven from the inside out. Essence is about one's purpose, values, beliefs, and vision.

Essence describes who the leader wants to *be* to his or her followers— the example the leader wants to set. Bill George, in his book *True North: Discover Your Authentic Leadership,* writes about having a compass that guides a leader successfully through life. The first step is to understand yourself, who you want to *be* as a leader. To support this, George cites a study where seventy-five members of the Stanford Graduate School of Business Advisory Council were asked to recommend the most important capability for leaders to develop; their answers were nearly unanimous: self-awareness. George refers to self-awareness as finding one's True North, the essence of leadership.

Meanwhile, *form* refers to what a leader needs to *do*—the behaviors and actions taken that demonstrate leadership competencies and are often driven by organizational expectations and norms. Form comes from the outside in and is the image or persona the leader creates by what he or she does.

Integrity is the integration between who one is and what one does—essence and form. Both are important to leadership, but more important is keeping essence and form in balance. In some situations, essence and form get out of balance. Think about the leaders you have encountered. Have you ever been around a leader who is form-oriented with little essence? How would you describe that experience? If a leader overemphasizes form over essence, he or she can be described as looking the part, but not acting it, being politically correct with the right people, or managing upward to please the boss rather than being focused on leading employees. On one occasion, an employee described a leader in the following manner; "If you take the suit off, there is nothing there." When form is overemphasized, a trust or credibility gap can arise because employees don't see the leader's character. Employees don't feel the leader is being authentic. The question for leaders to answer is: "Where do you get your signals that influence and shape you as a leader, from inside (essence) or outside (form)?"

> *The question for leaders to answer is "Where do you get your signals that influence and shape you as a leader, from the inside or the outside?"*

The following chart summarizes the key differences between looking to external or internal sources to guide your leadership:

External	Internal
▪ Lack of "essence" qualities	▪ Clear on "essence" qualities
▪ Appearance more important	▪ Depth more important
▪ Responds to signals from others	▪ Responds to values
▪ Measures success by appearance, position, and title	▪ Measures success by effectiveness and contribution to others
▪ Life is lived on "approval"	▪ Life is lived on "purpose"

Understanding the importance of leading from an internal orientation is critical for leaders who are challenged by how to help employees reengage following organizational change.

> We have observed too many organizations select leaders for their charisma instead of their character, their image instead of their integrity, and their experience rather than their substance.

Changing one's perspective of leading

When we ask managers or leaders, particularly newer ones, what they need to be effective as a leader, they'll often start by describing what they think they need to *have.* They'll describe the need for power, authority, responsibility, control of the budget, and more. When we ask them if they had those things then what would they *do,* they say they would make decisions, set goals, and guide performance. Continuing on, we ask if they did those things, what would they *be*? They usually say they would be successful, promoted, valued, and so on. We refer to this perspective of leading is *having-doing-being.* The emphasis is on what a leader feels they need to *have.*

Our experience with effective leaders—most likely similar to the individuals you selected as your best leader—actually reverse the order. They start with what they want to *be* as a leader. They discover their purpose, identify their values, and think deeply about what leadership is. What they want to *be* as a leader then guides what they need to *do* and what they need to *have.* They discover they really don't need to *have* many of the things they thought they needed—power, authority, control—in order to be effective as a leader.

When you view leadership from a *being-doing-having* perspective, you see the signals that guide one's leadership are internally driven. It's important to restate and summarize the logic of the two orientations.

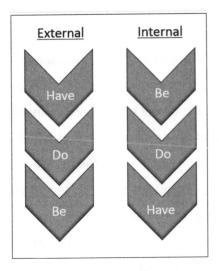

With an external orientation toward leading, the following logic occurs: "When I *have* enough (power, influence, control), then I'll be able to *do* the kind of things (direct, build, organize) that I've always wanted to do and I'll *be* (happy, rewarded, successful, recognized)."

With an internal orientation toward leading the following occurs: "Who am I? What do I want to *be* as a leader? After I have a sense of my purpose, beliefs, values, and vision, then I'll know what I'll need to *do* and know what I need to *have*."

Essence-based leadership

Being essence-based, or leading from within as we like to describe it, is essential for reengaging an organization for four key reasons:

1. Reengagement requires the leader to set the example.
2. Reengagement needs leadership resiliency.
3. Reengagement calls for leadership courage.
4. Reengagement requires the leader to practice mutual influence.

Leading by example

Think back to The Choice Model in chapter one. We shared the research that during periods of discontinuous change, a high percentage of employees make the choice to be inactive, ranging from pseudo complying to waiting and seeing or even unplugging. When asked what they needed to reengage, one of the core themes was leadership's example. What follows is a story of what can happen when leadership fails to understand the power of leading by example.

Tom worked with a group of highly successful sales leaders employed by a large, successful high-tech organization. They measured success in terms of producing results, not their effectiveness as essence-based leaders.

Tom presented this task to them: "Think about your definition of leadership and what you believe is required to lead. Now assume you're asked to present a five-minute talk on your leadership philosophy and beliefs to a group of newly hired managers at their orientation session. Outline your presentation."

To everyone's surprise, Tom then asked each of them to stand and deliver their speech in front of their peers. Out of fifteen participants, only three seemed to have seriously ever thought about this and could articulate their beliefs about leadership. Tom realized the remaining twelve had put little, if any, thought into understanding what leadership is about. Their rambling, cliché-filled statements were a hollow echo of "the things to say," rather than the passion and conviction that comes with "the things I believe." They were in positions of leadership, but they didn't think like leaders.

As a follow-up to the story, the organization, like many, began to experience a downturn in sales. Many of the high-achieving and well-paid sales executives became disengaged and left the organization. It's an oversimplification to say the lack of leadership was the cause of the turnover, but Tom had no doubt it was a contributing factor.

Arguably the most important role leadership can play is to bring positive energy and engagement to the workplace. According to Jim Loehr and Tony Schwartz in their book, *The Power of Full Engagement,* leaders are the stewards of organizational energy. They define full engagement as the "skillful management of energy focused on high performance." This next example is a positive one from a leader who truly understood the power of leading by example.

Several years ago Steve had the opportunity to work with Motorola. He had developed a leadership journal for Motorola called *Leading From Within,* the use of which was occurring in small areas of the company. The journal focused on the question: Who do you want to *be* as a leader? Most of Motorola's emphasis at the time was on what leaders should *do*. The journal focused on the leaders' qualities—purpose, values, vision, strengths, character. The president of Motorola at that time was Robert Galvin, who many in the organization held in high esteem for his essence-based leadership qualities and practices. After reviewing the journal, he publicly held it in front of a gathering of Motorola employees and said, "This is what leadership is about." Needless to say the requests for the journal increased significantly. Galvin shared his thoughts and beliefs about leadership, and from his insights and influence, Steve developed a definition of leadership that captures the transformational role of a leader:

> Leadership is the ability to take others to a place they would not go by themselves, not by the power of the leader's position, but by the strength of the leader's example.

We break down this definition here to help you better understand what it means:

- *Ability* is the knowledge and competence to lead.
- *Others* refers to those who call a person their leader. This definition of leadership doesn't apply to a position or title but rather anyone in a position to influence others.
- *Place* refers to a higher standard of performance, a desired outcome, or a different way of approaching something. Any time leaders chose to initiate change, they're attempting to take the employees to a different place. *Place* is a call to action.
- *Not by the power of the leader's position, but by the strength of the leader's example* recognizes the importance of leading by example rather than using one's authority, power, or control to engage the organization. Remember a leader is always making an impact, positive or negative, but rarely neutral.

A person given the title of president, vice president, director, or manager is in a position of authority and responsibility. This title, however, doesn't make the person a leader. Having a position of authority typically provides two benefits: compliance and attention. Because of a person's authority or title, employees will typically do what the leader asks them to do. They have learned to take direction or to follow orders. Employees will comply, often willingly, but at other times grudgingly. Compliance is different from commitment. Compliance is a "have to." Commitment is a "want to."

Being in a position of authority also brings the leader attention. The leader is attended to. The leader's constituency is constantly watching him or her. Employees look for signals that reveal who the leader is and what the leader plans to do. They look for signals that tell them how they should follow and what they should do. For example, if employees pick up signals that the leader isn't engaged in a new initiative, they will often choose not to be engaged. If the leader is resisting change, the employees feel they have permission to resist the change as well. If the leader is engaged, they will be more apt to be engaged. Whether the leader wants to be or not, he or she is being watched and is therefore, *always setting an example,* and the employees are talking about that example. Therefore, a critical question for leaders to ask themselves every day is, *"What do I want my example to be?"*

> **As a leader, if you want to influence the choice of employees to reengage, ask yourself, "What does my example need to be?"**

Leaders who give energy to the organization work extremely hard to create a *committed* following with their influence and example.

Leadership Resiliency: Leader as Pathfinder and Steward

What comes to mind when you think of fabric that is resilient? Something that is flexible yet durable? How about elastic yet tough? Similarly, a resilient leader needs to strike a balance between being flexible and durable—in other words, between *pathfinding* and *stewardship*.

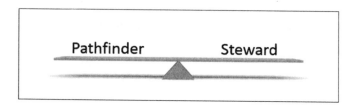

As a pathfinder, a leader is expected to continually change or renew that part of the organization for which he or she is responsible, working on ways to make things better, more effective, or different. Being a pathfinder calls for taking others to a place they wouldn't go by themselves. Employees want their leader to lead.

Especially during times of change, where disengagement is likely, employees want to see their leader setting the example from the front rather than leading from behind.

On the other hand, as a steward, the leader is expected to protect constants—what doesn't change. While being a pathfinder is about creating change, stewardship is about protecting those enduring tenets that shouldn't change. These tenets include the leader's values, purpose, and vision. This is about the strength of one's example. When change is about to disrupt the organization, important questions a leader, with input from employees, has to answer include the following: "What don't we change?" "What is too important to change?" or, "As we go through change, what do we want to bring with us?" Strong leaders stay the course and don't let the daily/weekly/monthly roller coaster of business take them off the path.

Knowing what needs to be changed and what needs to be held constant (too important to change) is always an act of balance and foresight.

> *"In matters of style, swim with the current.*
> *In matters of principle, stand like a rock."*
> -Unknown

Leadership Courage

> *"Unless we stand for something, we shall fall for anything."*
> -Peter Marshall, Senate chaplain, April 18, 1947

In our research with employees regarding what it would take to reengage, a theme frequently heard was "leadership's example." We then asked the question, "What are you looking for in a leader?" The two most frequent responses were "integrity" and "courage." When asked about courage, the description of what employees were looking for was less about the "courage of doing" and more about the "courage of being."

In today's complex, rapidly changing global business environment, hard choices need to be made, difficult decisions need to be implemented, and consequences for wrong choices can be devastating. In this kind of environment, demonstrating courageous leadership becomes more important than ever. The question is "Where does your courage to lead come from?" Again, essence-based leadership provides the answer.

The Oxford American Dictionary defines courage as "the conviction to act on one's beliefs." Leadership requires acting in a courageous manner on matters that aren't always easy or popular. What allows you to be courageous? Be clear on what you stand for: your values, philosophy, and beliefs, which we have referred to as the essence qualities. Living life in response to one's values, measuring success by effectiveness and contribution to others, and living life on purpose provides the foundation upon which to lead courageously.

If you get your signals from external sources, then you tend to waver in the wind and are subject to doing things to meet others' approval, which is always subject to change. Taking leadership action based on external sources suggests that in order to get people to follow you, you must get them to like and approve of you. However, the reality is people tend to follow leaders who are true to what they believe in and act consistently on those beliefs, even when their actions may not be popular. In matters of principle, they stand like a rock.

Mutual Influence Relationships

Several years ago we had the pleasure of working with David Bradford and Allan R. Cohen, authors of the book, *Managing for Excellence: The Guide to Developing High Performance in Contemporary Organizations.* We were in the process of developing a workshop based on their work, and one of the most compelling things we learned from them in the area of leadership is the concept of mutual influence. We went on to define mutual influence in the workshop as follows:

> *"Mutual influence means that each person can influence the ideas and behaviors of others. A mutual influence relationship is an open working relationship in which both individuals are encouraged to speak freely, challenge each other, and hear and accept what the other offers."*

My ability to influence you is directly tied to my willingness to be influenced by you.

The big learning for us from this idea of mutual influence is that your ability to influence others is directly tied to your willingness to be influenced by others. Think again back to chapter one where we defined engagement as positive perception of what is being asked of the employee and high discretionary energy being given by the employee to make the changes happen. We also introduced the Choice Model that talks about the fact that people have a choice to be engaged or not. You can't make them be engaged; you can only influence their choice. As a leader in working to influence an employee to reengage, you'll most likely need to have some important and direct conversations about the employees' perception of what is happening in the organization and the level of energy he or she is willing to commit. If leaders want to increase their effectiveness in influencing employees to reengage, they must understand the power of mutual influence—the willingness to be influenced by others.

These three key questions are required by both the leader and the employee to develop a mutual influence relationship:

Mutual Influence Relationships – Three Key Questions

- Do we have commonality of purpose or intent?
  - *Are we really after the same thing?*

- Do we have others' best interests in mind?
  - *Do each of us trust that the other person truly cares about my interests?*

- Do each of us have information that will help us achieve what we both want?
  - *Do each of us have different information, or a different viewpoint that could help the other person succeed?*

The importance of mutual influence relationships to reengagement

If you can answer yes to all three of these questions, then you have the power to engage in a mutual influence relationship. There are some extremely important reasons why this kind of a relationship is important for leaders trying to keep employees engaged or helping them choose to reengage.

Leaders can't just talk employees into reengaging by imposing their thinking or the organization's thinking on them. Difficult and challenging dialogue must take place to help employees reengage. Leaders must allow employees to openly and honestly share their own perceptions about what is occurring and the employees need to be comfortable disclosing the impact those changes are having on them personally. If employees don't believe you have commonality of intent or don't have their best interests in mind, they won't open up and share their honest perspectives about the situation. Without understanding the true perspectives of the employees, leaders can't possibly know what information is most helpful to those employees when choosing to reengage or not.

The importance of balance

By definition, *mutual interest* is the ability of a leader to influence others and in turn the willingness to be influenced by them. This can get out of balance. A good example is what we have witnessed working with leadership teams. If the leader of the team using his or her authority and position overinfluences the team, over time, the team begins to say yes when the team wants to say no. The team remains uncomfortably quiet, which the leader reads as acceptance, when in fact the team has lost its voice. Because of the power of the leader's personality, the team complies. The team members have become bobbleheads. After the meeting has ended, these same team members will discuss among themselves their opinions, including what should have been said, their lack of commitment to what was decided, and their dismay with the leader. On the other hand, the leader believes his or her message was heard and agreed to.

A team can overinfluence a leader as well. If the team overinfluences the leader so he or she feels compelled to acquiesce to the team members' wishes, over time, he or she is saying yes when he or she should be saying no. If this dynamic persists, the leader loses his or her role in making decisions and loses his or her voice.

The key to a successful team is the ability to influence each other. When leading a team, consider the following questions:

- Do each of us share mutual interest?
- Do each of us listen to learn and understand?
- Do you balance the leader's influence on the team and in turn the team's influence on the leader?

Mutual influence: Lessons learned at home

The importance of mutual influence was driven home to Tom in an incredibly unexpected way—by his son, who was about ten years old at the time. As Tom tells the story:

I had come home from work following one of those days where it felt like the whole world was beating me up. All I wanted to do was to get home, take my shoes off, sit down, pet the dog, and relax. Instead, I didn't realize a wait-until-your-father-gets-home moment was waiting for me. I was informed of a number of things my son had, or hadn't done, and that he wasn't listening and I needed to talk to him. So, instead of calmly walking down the hall, sitting on the bed with him, and in my best father/coach way pointing out the error of his ways, I did what many frazzled parents do (I'm not saying I'm proud)—I stood in the kitchen and yelled at him to come out of his room. From there I proceeded to inform him how disappointed I was with his lack of responsibility, his unwillingness to listen, blah, blah, blah, blah, blah.

My son stood in the hallway, put his hands on his hips, and said, "You don't have to yell" and went back into his room. If you thought I was frazzled before, now I was really upset. But after all I'm an expert in this area, so I quickly analyzed the situation and concluded two things: he obviously didn't hear me and he didn't believe I was serious. Of course, the solution to that was to get loud and sarcastic.

So I yelled something to the effect of, "Oh I see, you don't do this and you don't do that, and then when I try to talk to you about it, you can't deal with it, huh?"

Convinced he would surely now get the point, my son walked back out into the hall and said, "It's not that I can't deal with it. I just hate being yelled at," and he walked back into his room.

To say that I was upset was an understatement. Before I could calm down and talk with my son, I started thinking about why I was so upset. I went back to my training in Rational Behavior Therapy to check my self-talk and ask myself what my beliefs were that were contributing to such a strong emotional reaction and what my intentions were regarding the way I was handling the situation. I realized one of my beliefs was that I wanted my son to be a well-behaved child, and at that point he wasn't. I also believed it was my job to correct him in a way that strengthened our relationship, not damage it. The more I thought about it, the more I realized I wasn't doing a good job of getting what I wanted and that helped me calm down and rethink my approach.

Now for those of you interested to know how the story ended, Tom calmed down and worked things out with his son. More importantly, the exchange got the two of us thinking about the whole concept of mutual influence. The first thing we did was to go back to the beliefs Tom shared that got him so worked up. We then discussed what Tom, at the time, believed his son's intentions were. He felt his son was being disrespectful and avoided taking responsibility for his actions.

Then the big breakthrough in our thinking came. We considered this idea about his son: "What if instead of thinking his intentions were to be disrespectful and avoid responsibility, they were identical to Tom's—he wanted his dad to be a good dad, and at that point he wasn't, and it was up to him to help him see that?" Now to be clear, neither of us believed at ten years old Tom's son was that mature or insightful to believe that, but what if it were in fact true?

When you understand and embrace the concept of mutual influence, you learn quickly that differences in positions, titles, or levels in a hierarchy aren't the most important thing in a relationship—even when one or more is present. Ask yourself these questions: Do you honestly believe you share the same intention? Do you truly care about each other? Do you have information that will help each other? If the answer to all three questions is yes, then you can learn to share that information in a way that helps both of you get what you want.

Having a belief in mutual influence relationships is more of an essence quality. In a later chapter, we will offer some ideas of how you can use collaborative communications skills to help you with the form side of mutual influence.

Chapter Summary

Leaders inspire or demoralize others first by how effectively they manage their own energy, and secondly by how well they mobilize, focus, invest, and renew the collective energy of those they lead. Wilson Learning Worldwide, the organization that Tom leads, suggests that the purpose of leadership is to engage others in committing their full energy for the creation of value and success. The means to do so are the practices embedded in the five elements that make up the majority of this book.

Arguably, how the organization is led determines success. How the organization behaves has at its core how leadership sets the example. As a leader, you need a compass that guides your leadership. The first step is to understand yourself, who you want to *be* as a leader, and then understand what you need to *do*—the behaviors and actions taken that lead others to a place they wouldn't go by themselves. The next five chapters focus on what to do, not through your position power or authority, but by your example. To reengage the organization, you need to be the example, serve as both pathfinders and stewards, demonstrate courage, and practice mutual influence.

C. William Pollard, former chairman of ServiceMasters, provides an excellent summary regarding the role of leadership: "Will the leader please stand up? Not the president or the person with the most distinguished title, but the role model. Not the highest-paid person in the group, but the risk taker. Not the person with the largest car or the biggest office, but the servant. Not the person who promotes himself or herself, but the promoter of others. Not the administrator, but the initiator. Not the taker, but the giver. Not the talker, but the listener."

This is what engages the employees of an organization.

In the next chapter, we'll explore the first of the five elements of engagement: The Element of Perceived Opportunity.

Chapter 3

The Element of Perceived Opportunity

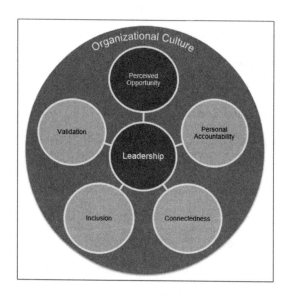

Premise: **Engagement occurs when employees feel they are part of something important, when they feel that what they are doing has purpose, when they can clearly link their purpose to organizational direction. Engagement begins when employees buy into something.**

In chapter one, we introduced you to Avcor Technologies as our business case. One of the prominent ways those employees had experienced loss was related to hope for the future. Most employees thrived in the old culture where they felt like their work had purpose and the future was promising. They were excited about being involved in opportunities. After that sense of future was lost, so too was their energy. Many employees left to find that feeling again in another organization.

A few years ago, we had the opportunity to work with a large insurance company in Massachusetts that had acquired a similar company operating in Connecticut. The acquired company had been experiencing a significant decline in market share and was facing the possibility of going out of business. The acquisition by a healthy firm seemed to be the perfect solution.

Both companies were well aware the acquisition would result in significant layoffs for the acquired company, because many of the services could be integrated into the acquiring company's existing business model. The question became how to best approach the pending downsizing. The decision was made to first offer generous severance packages and see how many Connecticut-based employees would voluntarily leave. If not enough employees took the package, the acquiring company would then initiate a formal layoff process. The target was to reduce the workforce by about four hundred employees.

What was unknown to the acquiring company was the story that the Connecticut employees were living within prior to the acquisition. Employees were made to feel their company had no future, that it was only a matter of time before it closed the doors. The employees had lost hope. Although one would think the news of an acquisition would restore some of their energy, instead the employees focused on the reality that many of them would lose their jobs.

When the acquiring company offered the severance package, about six hundred employees chose the package. Now, the company had a different dilemma to deal with. Too many individuals wanted to leave. Few wanted to stay. The impact on both organizations was significant and costly. The incentive to leave was a generous severance package, and staying seemed to offer little hope. Employees had been sold on the choice of leaving rather than staying. Those who did stay were left in a state of confusion about whether they had made the right decision. In many cases, they chose to disengage and take a wait-and-see attitude rather than fully engage. In addition, the employees were "rewarded" with more work to do and fewer people to do it.

What is the lesson? Leaders who are sponsoring change to effectively manage the transition must communicate realities and take care of their constituency. There are varying points of view on how to do this.

John Kotter, in his book, *Leading Change: An Action Plan from the World's Foremost Expert on Business Leadership,* spoke of creating a sense of urgency or motivation about the change the organization wants to initiate. This can be accomplished in two basic ways: speaking to the problems or challenges or speaking to the opportunities. In the preceding business example, most employees only heard about the problems.

Speaking to the Problems

Speaking to the problems focuses primarily on the current state of the organization, on what isn't working. Examples could be poor fiscal performance, increased competition, high operating costs, a looming downturn, and so on. Kotter recommends identifying potential threats and then developing scenarios that show the gravity of the situation and what could happen in the future.

Daryl Conner, in his book, *Managing at the Speed of Change: How Resilient Managers Succeed and Prosper While Others Fail,* used the term "standing on a burning platform" as a way to describe how to motivate employees to accept necessary change. The story behind the term was based on the 1988 Piper offshore oil rig fire in the North Sea off the coast of Scotland, considered the worst offshore oil disaster in history in terms of lives lost. The purpose of the story was to show how to encourage employees to act because of an impending crisis or the strong likelihood that the business environment would deteriorate if the current course continued. The idea being that uncovering the problems with the organization's current state would motivate employees to embrace change.

Nokia CEO Stephen Elop wrote a memo describing his company's situation. Although not a recent story, it provides a great example of how to employ the burning-platform analogy to articulate a sense of distress or urgency to act. Here are parts of his speech to the company's employees:

There is a pertinent story about a man who was working on an oil platform in the North Sea. He woke up one night from a loud explosion, which suddenly set his entire oil platform on fire. In mere moments, he was surrounded by flames. Through the smoke and heat, he barely made his way out of the chaos to the platform's edge. When he looked down over the edge, all he could see was the dark cold, foreboding Atlantic waters.

As the fire approached him, the man had mere seconds to react. He could stand on the platform and inevitably be consumed by the burning flames. Or he could plunge 30 meters into the freezing waters. The man was standing upon a "burning platform," and he needed to make a choice. He decided to jump. It was unexpected. In ordinary circumstances, the man would never consider plunging into icy waters. But these were not ordinary times, his platform was on fire. The man survived the fall and the waters. After he was rescued, he noted that a "burning platform" caused a radical change in his behavior.

We too are standing on a burning platform, and we must decide how we are going to change our behavior. Over the past few months, I've shared with you what I've learned from our shareholders, operators, developers, suppliers, and you. Today, I'm going to share what I've learned and what I have come to believe.

I have learned that we are standing on a burning platform. And we have more than one explosion—we have multiple points of scorching heat that are fueling a blazing fire around us. For example, there is intense heat coming from our competitors, more rapidly than we ever expected. Apple disrupted the market by redefining the smartphone and attracting developers to a closed, but very powerful ecosystem. In 2008, Apple's market share in the $300+ price range was 25 percent; by 2010 it escalated to 61 percent. They are enjoying a tremendous growth trajectory with a 78 percent earnings growth year over year in Q4 2010. Apple demonstrated that if designed well, consumers would buy a high-priced phone with a great experience and developers would build applications. They changed the game, and today Apple owns the high-end range. . . .

While competitors poured flames on our market share, what happened at Nokia? We fell behind, we missed big trends, and we lost time. At that time, we thought we were making the right decisions, but with the benefit of hindsight, we now find ourselves years behind. The first iPhone shipped in 2007, and we still don't have a product that is close to their experience. Android came on the scene just over two years ago, and this week they took our leadership position in smartphone volumes. Unbelievable.

He cites several examples of Nokia's own innovations, failing to bring them to market fast enough and having only a single product ready for market by the end of 2011. He talks about having another product that has proven to be noncompetitive. Later he states, "We have lost market share, we've lost mind share, and we've lost time."

His next point speaks to the possibility of significant rating downgrade by Moody and Standard & Poor's because of their concern for Nokia's competitiveness:

How did we get to this point? Why did we fall behind when the world around us evolved? This is what I've been trying to understand. I believe at least some of it has been due to our attitude inside Nokia. We poured gasoline on our own burning platform. I believe we have lacked accountability and leadership to align the direct the company through these disruptive times. We had a series of misses. We haven't been delivering innovation fast enough. We're not collaborating internally.

Nokia, our platform is burning.

We are working on a path forward—a path to rebuild our market leadership. When we have the new strategy on February 11, it will be a huge effort to transform our company. But I believe that together we can face the challenges ahead of us. Together, we can choose to define our future. The burning platform, upon which the man found himself, caused the man to shift his behavior and take a bold and brave step into an uncertain future. He was able to tell his story. Now, we have a great opportunity to do the same.

If you were sitting in the audience listening to Elop speak, what would be going through your mind?

Is focusing on the problem a way to engage employees? It depends. First, creating a burning-platform scenario is an effective strategy if it's based on realistic, factual information. The analogy isn't effective if it's based on emotional speculation or uses manipulated information to manufacture the severity of the organization's current reality.

Secondly, although a burning-platform scenario creates a sense of urgency, it also has the potential of creating in the minds of the employees the belief that they're part of the problem rather than part of a solution.

The result is potentially leaving employees feeling demotivated and having them wonder what the scenario may mean to them personally.

Thirdly, if the burning platform is overplayed, the consequence may result in people leaving for better situations or opportunities rather than staying and helping the organization change. We don't recommend you use a burning-platform scenario, like the insurance company unintentionally created when it offered a generous severance package. The result is typically significant, unintended consequences. It's a good strategy in the right situations, but it's accompanied by a level of risk, depending on what employees read into the scenario. Focusing on the problem can just as easily disengage employees rather than engage them.

Speaking to the Opportunity

Kotter also suggests in order for change to be successful, seventy-five percent of a company's management (we would say this percentage applies to employees as well) needs to buy into the change. The question becomes: "Can you build urgency by focusing primarily on future opportunity rather than current problems?" We believe the answer is definitely yes.

This is where the element of perceived opportunity comes in. The research with organizations in our survey suggests the following:

> The mindset that best serves full engagement is realistic optimism—working positively toward a desired outcome or solution.

Employees need to believe in the future and understand how they fit in. They need to see potential in order to give the organization their energy. Having a clear why for each change increases the probability that employees will choose to stay engaged or to reengage.

Realistic Optimism

Realistic optimism is truthfully sharing problems associated with the organization's current reality and most importantly moving to a focus on how to create a positive future.

> A key to reengagement is to establish a positive and realistic belief in the future—a perceived opportunity.

To enhance the element of perceived opportunity, leadership needs to create a message of realistic optimism. Realistic optimism doesn't sugarcoat the problems that exist; it moves the focus away from the problems and creates a sense of optimism about where the organization needs to go or what leadership wants to accomplish. Elop, in the Nokia example, did this only as a summary statement:

We are working on a path forward—a path to rebuild our market leadership. When we have the new strategy on February 11, it will be a huge effort to transform our company. But I believe that together we can face the challenges ahead of us. Together, we can choose to define our future. The burning platform, upon which the man found himself, caused the man to shift his behavior and take a bold and brave step into an uncertain future. He was able to tell his story. Now, we have a great opportunity to do the same.

By that time, Nokia employees may have no longer heard the message of opportunity if they had become overwhelmed with the details of the problem.

Preparing a statement of realistic optimism—the how of perceived opportunity

The most basic way to prepare a statement of realistic optimism is to complete the following statements:

- Looking forward, what worries you the most?
- Looking forward, what excites you the most?

Don't reverse these two questions by starting with the second question first. Balance the content of the two questions, favoring what is exciting about the future. With the information from these two questions, write a simple statement of realistic optimism that describes a positive picture about the future for your specific constituency.

The message has to feel real to people, not just "rah, rah" or "we're going to be the greatest." The leadership is responsible to clearly articulate to employees the reality they and the company are operating within. Be real. That's what employees want. Presenting only a positive picture when everyone knows when problems exist can create the impression that leadership isn't being truthful with them.

The power of communicating realistic optimism

Working with a global organization in the services industry, we had the opportunity to experience the power of realistic optimism. The company had once been an industry market leader with widely accepted products and services, a strong customer base, and many long-term employees. The organization experienced growth and profits for many years running. However, following the 2008 economic crisis, the company's customers began to drastically cut budgets. The company's contracts were some of the first to be cut by its customers, and even when the economy picked up, the company's contracts were among the last to be reinstated.

Company executives responded by shifting their focus from growing the business to focusing on not failing. Investment was curtailed, employees were laid off, and performance pressure on the sales force increased. The organization began to experience bottom-line losses, and many of its long-term, talented employees who had helped build the business left. The cumulative effect was an organization that unplugged. Compared to the high energy of the past, the office felt like a morgue when we walked through the headquarters.

We were already working with the leadership team below the executive level, trying to create an approach to reengage the organization. However, when we met with these leaders, we found them to be chief among the discontented. They described themselves as still caring, but they were just plain frustrated and tired. The first thing they wanted to do was vent their frustration with the damage caused by the executives. After they had a chance to let off some steam, they agreed to focus on what they could do to help.

74

We asked them to answer the two questions related to realistic optimism:

- Looking forward, what worries you the most?
- Looking forward, what excites you the most?

Their answers to the first question validated that their concerns, and those of the employees, were legitimate. They feared if nothing changed the company would be out of business in three years. Whether it was true or not, that was their fear. Their answers to the second question about what excited them revealed they had many positive things going on and a lot to be encouraged about. But they confessed that the fear of the company closing tempered their excitement was tempered. They decided to stop focusing on "the burning platform" they felt they had been living on and begin "speaking to the opportunity."

These two questions allowed them to break the challenge of "How to save the company?" into smaller, more manageable actions. They felt confident they could share their concerns about the future with employees and still excite them about working on initiatives that had the potential to make a difference in the marketplace. Each leader identified key pieces that he or she owned and created action plans to implement those ideas within his or her individual areas. As a result, the leaders reenergized their employees, creating their future together.

Practices Related to Realistic Optimism

Several practices give an organization a sense of future, also referred to as a sense of perceived opportunity. These practices include the following:

Having a strong vision

A *vision statement* is sometimes called a picture of a company in a future state, but it's much more than that. A vision statement is leadership's inspiration, providing the framework for setting the goals needed to move toward the desired future state. When leaders create a vision statement, they're articulating their dreams and hopes for the organization. Doing so reminds employees of what they're trying to build or trying to become. A strong vision creates buy-in. In a visioning session with a large construction company, we posed questions to the senior leadership team and their general managers as the first step in creating the company's vision. Project yourself five years into the future and answer the following questions:

- What kind of reputation do we have in the industry?
- What kind of customers do we have?
- What perception of us do we want to have in our customers' minds?
- What kind of relationships do we have with our customers?
- When we are asked why we do what we do, what do we want our answer to be?
- What products and services do we see our customers using?
- What qualities do we see in our people?
- How are our people approaching their work?

- What does working smart look like?
- What innovations are occurring?
- How does our financial statement read?

We used the senior leadership team's and general managers' answers as the framework for creating a vision statement. This approach proved successful. First, it involved a number of leaders and managers rather than just one leader. Secondly, the collective input of several individuals proved more insightful than from just a small group. Thirdly, ownership and engagement was high, and participants felt like they had helped author the future.

It's important that a vision statement captures the passion of employees and leaves those employees feeling they're part of the future.

Creating a sense of mission

A *mission statement* declares the organization's purpose. It announces to the world at large what the company exists to do. Employees want to know the why of what they do. For example, Courtyard by Marriott's mission statement is as follows: "To provide economy- and quality-minded travelers with a premier, moderate-priced lodging facility, which is consistently perceived as clean, comfortable, well-maintained, and attractive, staffed by friendly, attentive, and efficient people."

This mission statement is effective because it identifies the primary Courtyard by Marriott customer (economy- and quality-minded travelers), explains what the hotel chain is (a premier, moderate-priced lodging facility), and clearly states what it provides (consistently clean, comfortable, well-maintained, and attractive, staffed by friendly, atten-tive, and efficient people).

Creating a sense of personal purpose

Richard Leider, author of *The Power of Purpose: Find Meaning, Live Longer, Better,* defines purpose as one's "reason for being, one's aim in life." Leider believes having purpose is the foundation of a meaningful life. Having purpose allows employees to put their own signature on their work. Having purpose can be experienced as creating something of lasting value—in other words, the feeling of adding something to their world.

You can find a more compelling reason to establish a sense of per-sonal purpose in the book, *Start with Why: How Great Leaders Inspire Others to Take Action,* by Simon Sinek. In studying the leaders who've had the greatest influence in the world, Sinek discovered they all think, act, and communicate in the exact same way, and how they communicate is completely the opposite of what everyone else does. Sinek believes pas-sion decreases and stress increases when leaders focus primarily on what and how their organization operates, rather than on why the organization operates. He contends that communicating the why is the connecting belief-element. It creates a sense of "purpose for being."

Setting organizational goals

Organizational goals set forth the methods by which the vision, mission, and strategy will be achieved. They also provide more specific measures that allow everyone to assess how the organization is doing. Goals also help answer the employees' question: "What do you expect of us?" We will discuss goals in greater detail in chapter four.

Realistic Optimism and Strategy Development

When exploring a strategy for moving the company forward, realistic optimism must meet certain criteria. The three criteria from the employee's perspective are:

1. Is the strategy believable?
2. Is the strategy doable?
3. Is the strategy feasible?

Employees and management need to buy in to what is being asked of them. If the majority of employees don't think the strategy is believable, it's likely that the strategy will meet some form of resistance or a wait-and-see posture.

Sometimes, the strategy is believable (a good idea), but it's not doable in the minds of the employees. They question execution when they can't see the strategy being accomplished for reasons of time, required expertise, complexity, and so on. If a percentage of the organization doesn't feel the strategy is doable, at best engagement will be some form of compliance: willful, grudging, or pseudo complying.

At times, the strategy is believable and doable, but not feasible. Management or employees question feasibility when the strategy is believable and doable, but the lack of money or resources will prevent execution.

When any one of the three questions remains unanswered or is a concern, the employees will likely choose to withhold their energy or grudgingly comply at best.

We participated in a pharmaceutical sciences meeting where a leader introduced a new supply chain process to the managers. The presentation of the process came across as too detailed and confusing to participants. There was little energy in the room as the leader finished presenting the suggested process. We asked if we could conduct a quick poll of the audience. We created three scales from one to five, with one being low and five being high. The first scale asked participants if they believed the strategy was a good idea. The second scale asked if they felt the strategy was doable. The third scale asked if the strategy was feasible.

The results were interesting. The majority of participants gave scores of three to four for believability and scores of four to five for feasibility. On the scale whether it was doable, they gave the strategy scores of one to two: employees had gotten lost in the complexity. If the leader had assumed everyone was on board after the presentation, the project could have easily failed because those who would have to execute the process had little energy. We shared the survey results with the team. With the employees' help, the process was made more doable. As the leader and the participants worked through the details, engagement increased significantly.

Communication is Key

While focusing on the previously mentioned practices is critical to creating a sense of realistic optimism, these applications aren't sufficient to enhance engagement. How leaders communicate and use what they've created is just as critical as what they created. The following example really drove home that concept for us.

We worked with a large, global, high-technology company that was a chip manufacturing market leader. The company launched a new division with the mission to create a completely new technology for the consumer electronics market. The new division was still in the research and development phase when trouble arose. The new division had experienced a high degree of turnover among extremely important, high-valued engineers. It had an internal culture counsel who conducted work-culture surveys and found a high level of "noise in the system" and low work satisfaction. We were invited to come in and work with the president (Bob) and his senior leadership team on what was described as a leadership-development initiative.

One of the first things we did was implement a multi-rater-feedback process, which showed the employees' biggest concern related to having a tangible vision. This news troubled Bob who had spent much of his time communicating the vision, mission, and goals of the new division and who had thought they were clear and compelling. After much discussion, he concluded, "Regardless of how much communication has taken place, it would seem the employees just aren't getting it." As you can imagine, he took it quite personally.

Bob could have easily assumed any one of the vision, mission, or goals wasn't clear or that the employees weren't buying in. Further investigation showed that wasn't the case. Bob was the only one giving the speeches about the new division's direction, and all of his communication focused on how important the new endeavor was to the organization. The presentations were essentially one way with no discussion. The engineers weren't reacting to the rightness or wrongness of the vision; they were just unclear about how they fit in. They weren't sure if they had been selected for a new special project or had been removed from the profitable mainline business. The more that Bob repeated the message, the more employees tuned out. They even nicknamed the vision, "Bob's vision."

Although the vision, mission, and strategy were exactly what the new division needed, no effort was being made to connect the engineers to the new direction. No one talked with them about how their individual contribution was critical to driving the strategy, nor about how they were a key part of the future and not being put out to pasture. Bob and his leadership team assumed the power of the new vision alone would inspire the employees.

We put together a plan where Bob would stop being the lone spokesman for the vision. We then involved his leadership team more in communicating the vision, mission, and strategy. The senior vice presidents began holding department meetings to explain how each department's function was critical to driving the strategy. Along with their managers they conducted one-on-one meetings with all employees, ensuring they all understood how they fit into the new plan and how their valuable skills contributed to the organization's success.

This approach proved to be the missing link. The organization didn't have the wrong vision, mission, and strategy. The problem was that Bob and his leadership team underestimated the amount of communication required to energize and excite the employees. Employees needed to feel a part of the future opportunity and where they fit individually. Turnover among the engineers dropped to zero, and the culture counsel reported that the "noise in the system" disappeared and employee morale scores improved. The bottom line: They achieved buy-in and reengaged the organization.

In addition to these previous practices, we want to add two other practices to help develop the element of perceived opportunity. The primary applications, which haven't been written about extensively, are as follows:

- Telling the organization's story
- Establishing an organizing principle

Telling the Organization's Story: The Three Stories

When working with an organization, the first meeting is often the most interesting. Usually within a short period of time, the leadership team members tell us their story, a description of what is currently taking place within the organization. Usually, we hear a variation of one of the following stories:

Story:	One: We're in crisis	Two: We're changing again	Three: What is our potential?
Questions on people's minds:	Can we survive?	Will the changes work?	How good can we get?
Feels like:	Only a matter of...	In-between times	Opportunity
Strategic focus:	Downsize Operating costs Alternative scenarios	Processes Structure Re-something	Growth Execution Effectiveness
Hope to accomplish:	Stability	Remain competitive through efficiencies	Sustainability Expect the best
Work satisfaction:	Decreases	Becomes unpredictable	Remains healthy
Talent:	Lives in the loss Quits and leaves Quits and stays	Gets burned out Puts energy on hold	Fully engaged Thrives

Story One: We are in crisis

When leadership is telling this story, the focus is typically some form of crisis, usually due to declining revenues and profits, lost market share, or a bleak future. The question on the employees' minds appears to be, "Can we survive?" The employees believe they are standing on a burning platform and it feels like it's only a matter of time before the doors close or before the company is sold or dismantled. This story expresses little hope in the future.

The strategy most often taken is to downsize, reduce operating costs, and develop alternative scenarios in case the current strategy fails, all of which are focused on stabilizing the organization, stopping the bleeding, or reversing a negative trend in order to live to fight another day. This strategy doesn't bring energy to the organization because each stabilizing act is most likely perceived as loss.

Employees are likely asking themselves:

- "How will this affect me?"
- "Will I still have a job?"
- "If I'm laid off, what will I do?"
- "How am I going to make ends meet?"
- "Where should I look for work?"

Rather than being engaged and trying to help reverse the downward trend, they're more likely to become disengaged.

Because of the experience of loss, work satisfaction decreases. Employees have lost their smile, and in many cases talented employees decide to leave, while others, maybe even more damaging, quit and stay.

Engaging the organization is difficult because manufacturing optimism for the future is hard. Little focus is on long-term strategy.

This story is difficult to address. Most often, as consultants we aren't invited to help because the last thing on leadership's mind is spending money on advice. When they need support the most, they often think they can't afford it.

Have you ever been a part of a scenario similar to Story One? If so, how was energy being used in the organization?

Story Two: The organization is changing again

Story Two is the most common narrative we hear. Conversation with the company's leadership often begins with "we're changing again." Leadership wants to talk about anticipated changes or the changes that are already occurring. To them, change is the new norm. Extended periods of relative stability no longer occur. They begin to believe change is the only constant. In this story, the question on most employees' minds is "Will the changes work this time?" They ask this question because they have likely witnessed much change that hasn't led to significant improvements, only a high degree of destabilization.

To employees, it can feel like in-between times, where everything is up in the air. Little stability exists. Many leaders are good at starting initiatives but not necessarily completing them. Some leaders think their role is to start things, and when an initiative is announced, their part is over. Often, the reason more change is needed is because the existing changes weren't executed well or weren't given an opportunity to develop before more changes were announced. These scenarios are the leading reason for disengagement attributed to change fatigue.

> Many leaders are good at starting initiatives but not necessarily at completing them.

The strategies most often employed in Story Two focus primarily on improving processes, eliminating redundancy, and playing with organizational structure. These efficiency efforts are directed at remaining competitive in the marketplace or avoiding moving back toward a crisis scenario like in Story One. We even had one employee describe his take on living in Story Two as, "Living in the land of Re." We had no idea what he meant, so we asked. He said, "It feels like I'm living in the land of Re because the organization is always 'Re-ing' something: restructuring, reprioritizing, reengineering, reinventing. . . I'm getting tired of it." This creates a sense of endlessness, and as we discussed earlier, it becomes a form of fatigue that ends with employees unplugging or disengaging.

As we discussed in chapter one, in this story of turbulence, personal energy disperses. Employees can easily become overwhelmed with too much to do and not enough time to do it. In many cases, employees put their energy on hold, choosing to wait and see. When change is frequent, the process of disengagement occurs over time.

Work satisfaction in Story Two is unpredictable. Some employees embrace the change because they see it as gain; their likely choice is to engage. Others are dissatisfied because they experience the change as loss; they'll likely disengage.

Story Three: How do we achieve our potential?

Leaders in Story Three want to talk about the organization's potential or the opportunities leading to a positive future. The question this leadership wants to focus on is: "How good can we get?" The message is about possibility and potential. The strategic focus is on growing the business and executing strategic initiatives. The focus is less on efficiencies and more on how the organization can be more effective. Profit is strong, and as a result more emphasis is placed on making the organization significant. Another common focal point is sustainable success—how to continue growth even during turbulent times. Leaders expect the best from their employees, and they want employees to be "all in."

Although efficiency is focused on doing things right (Story Two), effectiveness is focused on doing the right things (Story Three).

Within this story, work satisfaction tends to be positive because employees can see personal opportunities. Talent retention is high. This is a culture of full engagement because employees aren't problem focused; they're opportunity focused.

A large pharmaceutical company asked us to help determine why employees stayed in the organization rather than why they left. We conducted what became known as "stay interviews." One of the reasons employees stayed was referred to as the three Ps: pride, profit, and possibility. Employees stayed because they were proud of who they worked for and saw the organization as healthy and profitable, which, in their mind, opened up many possibilities for personal growth and career advancement. Although employees stayed for several reasons, the three Ps were an example of developing the element of perceived opportunity. Employees stayed engaged because they saw possibilities and how they fit in.

Consider these questions:

- Which story do you believe your organization has been telling?
- How has the story that is being told influenced the level of energy or engagement?
- Do you believe you are a permanent resident of Story Two, or is the organization using change to enable Story Three?
- Can your leadership speak to these three Ps in a manner that gives employees a sense of pride, a feeling of success and profitability, and the perception of possibilities?
- Which story do you want to tell?

Summary points of the three stories

If an organization's leadership is only focused on Story Two in order to avoid Story One, the organization will likely unplug over time. Stories One and Two are about problem solving, confronting current circumstances, and trying to change them. The actions tend to be reactive and the results do little more than fix something. The key is to stop focusing just on what has to change and start focusing on what the leadership wants to create.

Story Two often begins as an engagement process but quickly becomes energy draining if prolonged or repetitive. Over time, energy will tend to disperse and the population of employees will move toward burnout (unrecoverable fatigue) or put their energy on hold, eventually leading to the death of ambition.

Only Story Three truly engages employees. It's a story of potential, of "how good we can get." If a company is in Story Two, the key is to focus on using change as a means of reaching Story Three. Too often, organizations get stuck in Story Two, which feels like perpetual whitewater to employees.

Employees may be in Story Two while the organization is moving into, or is in, Story Three. For example, an organization may have a department that needs to implement a new or different process, which is a Story Two scenario, but is designing the future, which is part of a Story Three strategy.

> If the organization is already in Story Three, the key is to communicate and sustain it. If the organization isn't in Story Three, the focus should be on what it will take to get there.

The more that leadership can provide a Story Three message to employees, the more likely the message will result in a higher level of engagement, as long as the story is based on realistic optimism.

What do you do if employees have lost their energy because of a Story One or Story Two scenario? First, start by communicating a realistic Story Three message as the desired outcome. Share thoughts on the two questions: "What are you worried about?" and "What are you excited about?" Then, focus on some of the key themes found in Story Three: opportunity, effectiveness, potential, sustainability, and the question, "How good can we get?"

> Just asking the question, "How good can we get?" compels
> employees to seek answers.

Establishing an Organizing Principle

In his book, *Half Time: Moving from Success to Significance,* Bob Buford asks the question, "What's in your box?" He believes every person consciously or unconsciously organizes his or her life around what he or she metaphorically puts in the box. We use the term, "What's in your circle?" For example, a person could put success in his or her circle and organize his or her life around achieving it. Wanting to be successful begins to drive the decisions one makes and the aspirations one has and influences how time is used, priorities are set, and values are demonstrated.

Businesses also need to consider what they put in their circle, because consciously or unconsciously whatever is in the circle will drive the organization's energy. An *organizing principle* refers to what is put in the circle. What is in the circle is often reflected in what the organization uses to measure itself, what it pays attention to, what it talks most about, and what has the greatest effect on organizational behavior.

> *What do you believe your organization thinks most about, pays the most attention to, talks about, and uses as the principle measure of success?*

For example, many law offices have consciously chosen utilization, or billable hours, as their organizing principle. As a result, utilization becomes what is measured and talked about and will have a strong influence on employee behavior. Asking the lawyers to engage in activities that they view as reducing their ability to generate billable hours won't be well received and likely will get little energy. Utilization is what is in the circle and what will drive the focus of the members of the organization.

An organizing principle can also emerge unconsciously, yet still have the same impact on an organization's focus as a consciously chosen one. A colleague of ours in Bogota, Colombia, Dr. Alberto Perez, worked with a large, family-owned restaurant chain in South America. They were one of the first in the region to introduce an American-style hamburger restaurant to a culture of people who had no experience with that dining style. They worked hard to ensure all employees focused on creating a unique and fun experience for all of their customers, which were mostly families. The hamburgers were tasty and the customer experience was truly unique and special, which is what brought customers back again and again.

The owners decided to pursue a strategy of expansion and growth. They believed one of the keys to their strategy was to make all of the restaurants much more efficient. As a result, efficiency became the operating principle of the organization. They created new processes and standards to help drive efficiency and revised the training all employees received to focus more on being efficient. The metrics used to measure the regional managers and store managers were overhauled to reward efficiency. The result? Employees lost the why of their business. The customer was no longer the focus. Over time, the organization began to lose customers, resulting in a decrease in revenues and profits. Rather than expanding restaurants, they were forced to close some.

Dr. Perez worked with the owners to identify what used to be the organizing principle in their circle and what the organizing principle had become, even though neither one had been consciously chosen. They realized quickly that customer experience was the original answer but that efficiency was now in the circle. The focus had shifted away from the special customer experience they had been known for and had become obsessed with processes and cost reduction.

The owners gathered their leadership teams together, and with Dr. Perez's help, they created a plan for returning the organization's focus back to customer experience without losing some of the advantages of increased efficiency.

What do the law office and restaurant examples have in common?

- A company's organizing principle, whether consciously or unconsciously chosen, can have a major impact on how energy is used within the organization.
- The organizing principle doesn't replace the organization's vision, mission, or strategy. The legal firm's vision isn't to be utilized, and the restaurant's mission wasn't to be efficient.
- When an organization has unplugged, an organizing principle can become a way to focus on the future and reengage employees.

The purpose of an organizing principle

A major strategy for developing perceived opportunity is to agree on an organizing principle and then organize around it. For example, MEGlobal, a company focused on producing grinding media for the mining industry, chose the single word "quality" as the organizing principle in its circle for twelve months. With quality in the circle, the leadership created a set of thematic goals, which were listed as spokes or pillars, and they represented the ways leadership chose to promote, organize around, and measure against the principle of quality. The following figure illustrates it:

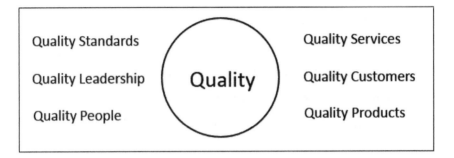

The leadership of MEGlobal wanted the organization to focus on six thematic goals and emphasize them when communicating to the larger organization. Each element became a benchmark toward making MEGlobal a quality organization. Some of the benchmarks, such as quality standards, quality services, and quality products, drove the technical emphasis of the business, whereas the others, quality leadership, quality people, and quality customers, emphasized what would be valued as part of the organization's culture.

These thematic goals became one of the key parts that MEGlobal used to build and tell its Story Three scenario, focusing on potential (how good can we get?). Employees bought into the importance of targeting all aspects of quality and chose to engage in making the organizing principle a way to focus their energies.

Declaring an organizing principle gives employees clarity regarding the organization's focus. Having the organizing principle memorable and part of the everyday language creates a sense of opportunity for the organization going forward.

Learning how to provide a Story Three scenario that visualizes where leadership wants to take the business, along with creating an organizing principle, helps develop the element of perceived opportunity. This is what engages or reengages employees.

What to consider when developing an organizing principle

To help identify which organizing principle should go inside the circle, leaders can ask these four focusing questions:

- What would get employees excited and engaged?
- What would give employees something to believe in?
- What is critical to helping the organization drive the vision/ mission/strategy?
- What does leadership want employees to think about, talk about, and measure against?

After leaders have identified the organizing principle, they can then identify the different thematic goals to energize and engage employees.

Chapter Summary

Leaders need to focus on creating what they want—the potential for the organization and its employees. Doing so gets employees believing in the future and to the organization's potential.

An organization can develop the element of perceived opportunity in several ways, including the following:

- Describing the future in the form of a compelling vision of the possible
- Having a strong mission statement so employees feel they're contributing to something larger than themselves
- Creating a real sense of purpose for employees, linked to the organization's mission and to the answer of why employees do what they do
- Developing a story focused on the organization's future and the question, "How good can we get?"
- Using an organizing principle or thematic goal as a way to consistently tell the story

In our next chapter, we will explore the next of the five elements of engagement: The Element of Personal Accountability.

Chapter 4

The Element of Personal Accountability

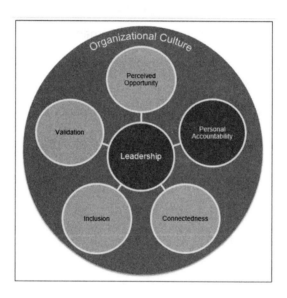

Premise: Engagement happens when employees are expected to give their best and know what they are being held accountable for. When this is the case, personal accountability increases.

In situations similar to Avcor, a primary reason for disengagement resulting from disruptive change is the loss of clarity. Employees lose sight of where the company is heading, what the new goals are, and what is likely to happen next in the organization's evolution. On a more personal level, employees become disoriented. In chapter one, we described disorientation as a high level of confusion, or lack of clarity about what's happening as a result of the changes. Typically, employees have many more questions than answers. They may feel their current situation is up in the air, chaotic, unclear, empty, or confusing. Struggling with how to move forward, they fail to commit to the new reality. They feel lost, they unplug, and they often choose to wait and see what will happen, seeking clarity regarding their role.

To reengage employees, leadership needs to focus on reorienting employees to their new reality by clarifying the organization's or department's direction, defining roles, and providing clear goals and expectations. This chapter focuses on how to create, or if engagement is currently high, how to sustain personal accountability. In doing so, employees know what the organization expects from them, what goals need to be met, and how to channel their energy going forward.

Clarify What You Expect of Me

In the research we did on what employees want from leadership to engage, one of the most common responses employees gave to the question, "What do you need from your leadership to reengage?" was, "Clarify what you expect of me." Employees want answers about the future, including what to focus on and what leadership expects of them.

Employees are more likely to reengage when they're clear on what they're being held accountable for. Accountability gives them a sense of direction. Accountability clarifies for employees where and how to focus their time and energy.

In researching this element of reengagement, we asked leaders from various organizations in our study group the following questions. As a leader, consider how you would answer the following:

- Is holding individuals personally accountable a strong leadership capability in your organization?
- How do you define personal accountability?
- From your perspective, what is the difference between a performance goal and an expectation?
- What demonstrates to you that an employee of yours is a future candidate to take your place?
- What would cause an employee of yours to not get promoted?
- What do you see happen in your work culture when employees don't know what is expected of them?

We found many interesting perspectives from the answers that leaders provided to these questions.

To the first question, the response was generally, "Well, not really." In all fairness, most leaders understand the concept of accountability and the importance of holding people accountable for their performance. What they told us, however, was that although many talked about accountability, they don't act on it as frequently or as consistently as they should. Many reasons may account for this, but we address two at this point.

Many leaders stated they believed if they gave clear directions, employees would carry out what was required. The problem with this belief is that providing directions or communicating goals may do a great job of starting the desired performance, but providing directions alone does little to sustain performance over time. After leaders have established directions and people have attempted to carry them out, leaders need to follow up with feedback and reinforcement to hold people accountable for continuing to perform as directed.

The second point connects to the first point. Many leaders cited the need to more clearly articulate what they expected from their people. Too often, leaders often assume people know what to do. In reality, they don't. Employees don't know how best to focus their energy, lacking a sense of what their priorities should be. The problem though is that cost cutting and downsizing often accompany discontinuous change that results in the loss of clarity. And in this environment, it's particularly difficult for employees to confess they have lost their focus and/or sense of what is expected of them. Leaders must engage in helping employees refocus, establish priorities, and set new goals and expectations.

Consider the following email Steve received from the president of an organization:

Dear Steve,

I hope all is well.

I wanted to speak with you regarding a concern I am noticing and get your thoughts. Overall we are falling short on our goals from a revenue, earnings, sales, and bookings perspective. When I speak with each of my business heads, they all seem concerned and mention they are trying, and they will look into the issues. However, we are not moving the ball forward. In fact, if you look at all the KPIs, we are moving backward.

To some degree I sense that folks are not focused on their goals and are too involved in other issues that take their attention away from where they need to be focused. I wonder if we can have a call to discuss a strategy regarding these concerns.

We recommended he provide better clarity regarding what the business heads would be held accountable for and review those account-abilities with employees more frequently. In addition, the business heads need to focus less on starting new initiatives and determine what they should stop doing that takes employees away from focusing on their goals.

Regarding the second question, "How do you define personal accountability?" the answers in most part were generalities: "Knowing what I am responsible for," "Taking responsibility for something," "Being held accountable," or "Being in charge." Because these answers were so general and vague, we decided to provide a clear definition of what exactly personal accountability is.

Personal Accountability

Personal accountability is present when employees are clear about what is expected of them from both performance goals and behavioral expectations.

Personal accountability is a product of both performance goals and behavioral expectations.

When employees are clear on what their leaders expect of them, they tend to hold themselves accountable. We heard from many engaged, high-performing employees who stated as soon they were clear on both performance goals and behavioral expectations, they knew what to do and didn't need their manager looking over their shoulder micromanaging them.

If an employee is clear on what personal accountability means, he or she might express it this way:

> I know what is expected of me. Because I have performance goals, I'm clear on how I'll be measured. Because I'm clear on what the organizational values are, I know the behaviors expected of me. Having both performance goals and behavioral expectations makes it much easier for me to hold myself accountable and monitor my own performance. Having that clarity and trust from my leadership really helps me stay engaged and energized.

Personal accountability gives employees the opportunity to answer, "How am I doing?" from a self-perspective. They're able to assess their performance against the knowledge of the goals and expectations being asked of them.

We're not saying leadership no longer has a role in holding others accountable. However, when the main source of accountability resides with the leader, the *locus of control* (refers to who is in control of providing the accountability) is an external source outside the employee. Having leadership create the conditions where employees increase their own sense of personal accountability, shifting the locus of control to the employees' own internal source, is much more effective. As we stated in chapter two, effective leaders get the signals that guide their behavior from internal sources. The same principle is in effect here.

> The ability to hold oneself accountable, and monitor one's own performance, is a stronger factor in an employee's reengagement than if accountability and feedback on performance come from external sources such as a manager.

Question three asked leaders, "What is the difference between a performance goal and an expectation?" Most leaders were unable to provide a clear explanation of what the differences are. In fact, many stated performance goals and expectations were more or less the same thing. Those managers used language like, "I expect you to complete the project on time and on budget," or, "I expect you to reduce costs by five percent in this year's budget." Instead of seeing performance goals and expectations as different, they saw expectations as part of how they communicated performance goals: "This is what I expect from you."

Steve and a team from Wilson Learning Mexico recently worked with the leadership team of a global conglomerate in the organization's Mexico City office. The organization had a new CEO who was brought in to take it to the next level. Many of its products were in mature markets, and the organization needed to shift its focus to emerging markets. The executive team initiated many changes and introduced new strategies and aggressive growth goals.

While Steve was with the executive level group discussing this topic of personal accountability, the executives were adamant that they had been clear about what was expected of the organization in terms of growth and the goals that needed to be accomplished.

At the same time an internal survey showed one of the biggest areas of concern was the lack of clarity regarding expectations. When executives discussed it with the middle management, they explained why they believed the lack of clarity of expectations was a problem. The middle managers said the executives were explicit about the goals they were expected to attain, but the executives provided no guidance regarding how they were expected to approach accomplishing the goals or the importance of why doing so was essential.

With all the changes and the new strategic focus, the middle managers didn't feel confident in what actions they needed to take and were unsure what their leaders wanted them to do. Therefore, they weren't certain how to reset expectations with their own direct reports. Rather than being energized by the new focus on growth, many employees became frustrated and began to unplug instead of performing in a way that helped drive the new strategy.

The executives were correct in their belief that they had communicated clearly what the goals were that the middle managers were expected to carry out. However, they only covered part of the equation if they wanted employees to hold themselves accountable for their performance. If the objective is to increase personal accountability, make sure you differentiate between a performance goal and an expectation.

The following helps clarify how we define performance goals and expectations:

Performance goals focus on achieving desired business outcomes. Well-written performance goals usually start with the word "to" followed by a verb (for example, increase), followed by a measurable outcome (face-to-face sales calls to five per week) and ending with a time frame (June 1). Check out these two examples:

- To increase face-to-face sales calls to five per week by June 1.
- To reduce machine downtime by ten percent by March 1.

Performance goals allow employees to clearly understand what they'll be held accountable for achieving. Performance goals are obviously nothing new and are a standard part of almost every organization. Establishing performance goals is part of the ongoing formal business planning process and serves as the foundation for performance reviews. Leaders are generally good at setting performance goals. In fact, how to set and communicate performance goals is often an important focus of entry-level management training. This book's purpose doesn't intend to teach leaders how to set more effective goals, but doing so is important to understand:

> Just having performance goals isn't enough to create a culture of personal accountability.

The other important aspect of personal accountability is less likely to be addressed in a formal manner: communicating behavioral expectations.

Expectations focus on expected behavior. Focus on two areas when clarifying behavioral expectations: performance focus and values focus.

<u>Performance focus</u>

Leaders need to connect expectations to a variety of performance-related activities. Examples include the following with examples to help you understand:

- **Corporate strategy:** Focusing on select vertical markets
- **Key corporate initiatives:** Increasing customer intimacy
- **Corporate goals:** Increasing revenue by five percent

After the leader has identified what he or she wants the employees to focus on at the organizational level (strategy, initiatives, goals), he or she then needs to ensure he or she is crystal clear on how employees should behave to drive those initiatives. Doing so doesn't mean overcontrolling or not empowering employees. The purpose is to provide clarity on what needs to be accomplished. Leaders can share their own expectations to help guide the employees' performance. In addition, an important way to empower employees is for leaders to have a dialogue with employees where they clarify what the employees will be held accountable for and get input from the employees regarding how they need to behave to achieve the goal.

The following are examples of how expectations might be linked to the performance goals that we previously mentioned:

Corporate strategy: Focusing on select vertical markets
• Establish criteria you'll use to analyze to focus on markets.   • Use resources we have paid for like Hoover's and ZoomInfo to research potential accounts.
Key corporate initiatives: Increasing customer intimacy
• Consider the customer's perspective when solving problems.   • Seek feedback from your customers to ensure their satisfaction.
Corporate goals: Increasing revenue by five percent
• Identify high potential target accounts within your selected vertical market.   • Prepare an account plan for your top three potential accounts.

Whether the leader provides behavioral expectations or discusses them with employees and then receives input to ensure that employees understand and agree to those expectations is important to employees being able to hold themselves accountable. The previous example of the global conglomerate illustrates the importance of having clear expectations for the performance goals but not having clear expectations for the behaviors needed to achieve the goals.

Values focus

The second area of focus for expectations relates to corporate values. Most organizations today have worked hard to identify and communicate the values most important to the organization. For example, values could be creativity, integrity, safety, and so on.

After leaders have identified what the corporate values are, they need to clarify expectations for how employees operationalize those values and behave consistently with them.

Wilson Learning has a set of beliefs and core values. Each of those core values has a list of expectations to guide employees to know how to behave consistently with those core values. The following is a small sample of the core values and expectations so that you may see the connection between the two:

We value collaboration and teamwork with our customers and throughout our global organization.
• We accept and support team decisions after they're made. • We acknowledge the value all team members' contributions. • We make decisions based upon business interests, not self-interest.
We value versatility and a win-win attitude when dealing with both colleagues and customers.
• We take steps to reduce interpersonal tension during an interaction. • We approach problems in a way that not only provides a solution, but also strengthens our relationships. • We seek solutions to problems that meet the needs of all the people involved.
We value having integrity, being personally accountable, and taking responsibility in our work lives.
• We meet commitments made to ourselves and to others. • We respond promptly to others' requests and keep them informed of our progress. • We accept responsibility for our own actions and admit our mistakes, take responsibility for our failures, and learn from both.

It's important for leaders to identify what they would expect to see someone do or hear someone say that would indicate the person is behaving in a manner that supports the organization's values. At that point, leaders need to clearly articulate to employees what their expectations are at a level of specificity that the employees don't doubt what they expect.

Remember: Leaders need a balance of clarity between performance goals and expectations that allows employees to take on more personal accountability.

In general, leaders have learned how to provide clarity on performance goals. The opportunity for improvement is often on the *expectations'* side of the equation.

> *Does your organization set expectations regarding how you want your employees to behave?*

Not only does setting expectations help your employees know how to behave, but it also increases your ability and the effectiveness of using consequences like rewards and behavioral correcting later when your employees either meet or don't meet goals and expectations. The more specific the goals and expectations, the more effective your consequences will be because your employee will know exactly what they did or didn't do to get either rewarded or corrected. Without that specificity, employees may know you're generally pleased or displeased, but they won't know exactly what behaviors they need to continue to do or to change.

We will go in to more detail later in this chapter regarding what leaders can do to ensure there is a better focus on both performance goals and behavioral expectations.

When leaders responded to question four, their answers primarily focused on qualities like trustworthy, loyal, insightful, people-oriented, natural leader, hardworking, collaborative, and hard charging.

Following these qualities and attributes, the second type of answer they gave us was in reference to their past performance: "Her group has the highest customer satisfaction scores in the department" and, "He proved himself to be a strong leader by introducing innovative process redesigns." Notice the first answers reflect more of an expectation focus and the second reflect more of a performance goal focus.

Add further to the responses to question four with the response to question five, "What would cause an employee of yours to not get promoted?" The reasons that leaders gave were most often behavioral: abrasive personality, uncooperative, poor listener, wasn't interested in meeting other people's needs, and so on.

We found it interesting that the standards used by leaders to determine if a person was a candidate for promotion or not were subjective, varying greatly from leader to leader. Although most organizations set up formal performance evaluation systems as a way to objectively evaluate if an individual had met predetermined performance goals, in general they were seldom referred to as the basis for promoting someone or holding someone back. Leaders described their assessment was based more on an individual's qualities, behaviors, and competencies.

More interesting is the observation that leaders often hire individuals based on the candidates' past performance as spelled out on their resume but fire them for their behavior.

> **Have you ever had an employee who performed well, but you had to fire him or her because of his or her behavior?**

Question six asked leaders, "What do you see occurring in your work culture when an employee doesn't know what is expected of him or her?" Let's expand on this issue by developing various scenarios that explain consequences when performance goals and behavioral expectations are or aren't present.

Personal Accountability Model

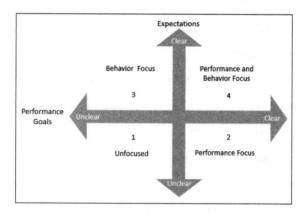

Performance goals and expectations can play out in four ways in an organization:

- **Quadrant 1:** This quadrant refers to having unclear performance goals and unclear expectations, which leads to employees being *unfocused*. It leads to a culture in which Joe Grabowski, former president of Wenck Environmental Engineers, describes employees as "floating in the ocean" or "just bobbing around."

- **Quadrant 2:** This quadrant refers to clear performance goals but unclear expectations. It leads employees to having primarily a *performance focus* (focused on performance goals and not on behavioral expectations). As a result, in this culture, employees focus on outcomes with few boundaries.

- **Quadrant 3:** This quadrant refers to clear expectations but unclear performance goals. It leads employees to having primarily a *behavioral focus* (focused on behavioral expectations, not on performance goals). As a result, employees focus on activities in this culture and not on outcomes.

- **Quadrant 4:** This quadrant refers to clear performance goals and clear expectations. It leads to employees having a *performance and behavioral focus* (focused on both performance goals and on behavioral expectations). This leads to a culture in which employees hold themselves personally accountable for both meeting performance goals and behavioral expectations.

Here, we explore each of the quadrants and illustrate possible scenarios.

Quadrant 1: Unfocused

What if the employees of an organization are unclear on their performance goals (what to achieve) and what is expected of them (how to behave)? When this is the case, employees often move to what we described as rust-out on the Energy Continuum in chapter one because they don't have high standards for performance to stimulate them, and their energy erodes over time.

The possible scenarios of disorientation are as follows:

In this scenario, employees have no direction. They proceed tentatively, hoping they're doing the right things. Steve recently spoke to an extremely competent employee of an organization who said, "I don't consider myself an employee of this organization. I haven't had a performance review by my manager in more than six years. Half of the time I do only what the job requires and the other half I just make it up."

A second scenario when employees become disoriented is similar to what Tom was told when he was young and living in Michigan: "If you get lost in the woods, stay in one place, don't move, and we will find you." From an employee's perspective, being lost in the woods means he or she chooses to do little, hoping someone will come along and provide the needed direction. With no direction, the employee may choose to quit and stay, using his or her energy to remain undiscovered.

A third scenario reflects on an employee's need to know how he or she is doing. Without the ability to measure oneself against performance goals, the employee is dependent on others to assess his or her performance. When they aren't provided feedback, employees often make assumptions regarding their performance and hope they're correct. Often with high-performing engaged employees, leaders may believe the employees don't need feedback and in essence are sending the message, "If you don't hear from me, then you're doing okay." High-performing employees want to know how they're doing. In the absence of feedback, they have been known to threaten to quit because that often prompts the leader to tell them how valuable they are.

Quadrant 2: Performance-focused

What if employees of your organization are clear on their performance goals, but they're unclear on what is expected of them? When this is the case, employees often learn the end justifies the means, or it doesn't matter how you do it, just get results. A classic example of this is when salespeople treat support staff poorly, and then justify their inappropriate behavior by pointing to their sales results as justification. Employees in quadrant two are often labeled as "not good corporate citizens."

At times, we have had the opportunity to sit in on senior leadership meetings as the leaders talked about various problems and challenges facing them. On more than one occasion, an employee's name has come up and the discussion has focused on the person's behavior. One such incident focused on a salesperson who was highly successful from a performance perspective, reaching all of his sales goals, but he flirted with the boundaries of ethical behavior.

Leaders described him as inappropriately spending company money, submitting expense reports that showed he was having extravagant meals, purchasing extremely expensive wine with existing or potential customers, and even staying in expensive New York City hotels even though he lived just outside the city.

Many on the team felt he should be fired because he exceeded the boundaries regarding expenses and he was setting a bad example for other sales personnel in the office. Yet others came to his defense, pointing out he made his numbers, and his spending beyond the norm contributed to his success. The team found it difficult to dismiss him when he contributed significant revenues to the organization. This conversation split the team. Tensions escalated, and no one reached a resolution during the meeting. About a year later the salesperson was let go for padding his expense account. The scenario regarding boundaries is a difficult one.

> *Do you reward performance and tolerate poor behavior, or do you hold everyone accountable for both performance and behavior?*

The dilemma this quadrant can present to the organization is often expressed as "winning at any cost;" if it comes at the cost of other employees, at the cost of the organizational values, or at the cost of others who want to play by the rules, so be it. Comments like, "He gets results, but he's hard on people," or "She is a good performer, but she doesn't work well with others" exemplify the dilemma of quadrant two. Setting behavioral expectations and boundaries are important to creating personal accountability.

> Leadership needs to determine where the boundaries are regarding how the employees represent themselves and how the employees represent the organization.

Quadrant 3: Behavior-focused

What if the employees of an organization are clear on what is expected, but they're unclear on their performance goals? When this is the case, employees often focus on doing activities, not on what their manager is expecting them to achieve or accomplish. Usually a behavior focus results in an uncomfortable performance review when the employee explains what he feels he has accomplished and the manager counters with her concern that expectations weren't met.

In this scenario, employee behavior is in line with the organization's values. Employees have a strong sense of how to interact with others and of what is important to the company. They'll likely be good organizational citizens, clear on how to behave, but unclear on how to perform.

Given the lack of direction regarding performance goals, employees will likely rely on what they assume or think they should be doing based on their job description. Employees may move forward under the assumption, "I'll perform my job as I understand it until I am told to do so or until given other directions." Employees will use a lot of their energy wondering whether they're doing the right activities or wondering how they're doing. When it comes to performance appraisal time, the manager can talk only in generalities regarding how employees are doing their job. The focus of the appraisal discussion will likely be on the qualities the employees demonstrate, not on meeting performance goals. How can employees be fully engaged if they don't have performance goals to strive for?

Does this quadrant's scenario sound a bit unusual? It's not. Many organizations have employees living in a world where they aren't clear on the specific ways of what and how they're being held accountable for performance. The sad part is the employees often have to rely on others to determine how they're performing. This scenario is another example of the locus of control being with external sources rather than with the employees, which reduces the employees staying engaged.

This scenario can result in employees being surprised and angered when the manager brings up areas in the performance review where they didn't perform up to the manager's expectations, yet they were unaware that they were being measured and evaluated in those areas.

Quadrant 4: Focused

What if the employees are clear on what is expected and clear on their performance goals? When that's the case, employees understand both the means and the ends matter and often exceed their manager's expectations. Their manager often seeks them out as a peer leader for how to get things done the right way. Employees in this quadrant often have the mindset of "Clarify what I am going to be measured on (performance goals) and what you expect of me (expectations), and then get out of my way and let me get to it. I don't need you standing over my shoulder driving me to excellence. I can take it from here."

The most important outcome of this scenario is the ability of employees to answer this question for themselves: "How am I doing?" If employees are clear on both performance goals and expectations, then they don't have to rely on the leader to provide the answer to this question. If clear performance goals and expectations are embedded in the culture, the use of performance reviews takes on a whole different meaning. In that case, the performance review is much more of a collaborative dialogue with the employees sharing with leaders how they're doing as much as the leaders sharing and reviewing. The employees have the ability to monitor themselves against stated goals and expectations.

When engaged employees hold themselves accountable, they often don't just meet expectations, they exceed them. They are a *conscious competent,* meaning they're good and they know why they're good, and they can critique their own performance while it's occurring, which allows them to better sustain their performance over time as well as adjust as needed to changing conditions.

To drive this point home, employees need to know what the opportunity is for them if they commit their energy to the goals and expectations that are being set for them. They want to know what is in it for them. We will discuss this in much more detail in chapter seven.

Expecting the Best: What It Means

The premise of this chapter is "Engagement happens when employees are expected to give their best and know what they are being held accountable for." When that's the case, personal accountability increases and engagement is evident.

The responsibility of leadership is to create a culture where personal accountability is a critical element. If disruptive change has resulted in disoriented employees, clarifying what they're accountable for in the form of performance goals and expectations reengages employees.

According to J. Sterling Livingston, a Harvard Business School professor who studied the Pygmalion effect in management (*Harvard Business Review*, September/October 1988), what leaders expect of their employees and the way they are treated largely determines the employees' level of engagement and performance. According to Livingston, "A unique characteristic of superior leadership is the ability to create a culture of high performance expectations that subordinates fulfill." He added, "We are all like Eliza Doolittle; we behave according to how we are treated."

Recall the Pygmalion effect from George Bernard Shaw's play *Pygmalion* (later the musical and movie *My Fair Lady)* that explores the notion that what is expected of another, for better or worse, can be transforming. Eliza Doolittle said in *Pygmalion:*

> You see, really and truly apart from the obvious things anyone can pick up on (the dressing and the proper way to speak and so on), the difference between a lady and a flower girl is not how she behaves but how she is treated. I shall always be a flower girl to Professor Higgins because he always treats me like a flower girl and always will. But I know I can be a lady to you because you always treat me like a lady and always will.

If you want the best, expect the best. In organizations, this means providing goals, setting expectations, encouraging people, and bringing out the potential in all employees.

Chapter Summary

It's important for leaders to value and understand the following:

- Performance goals are usually the focus of leaders' efforts, whereas in most cases, true engagement happens when both performance goals and behavioral expectations are clear.
- Leaders need to overtly articulate their expectations for employees and hold them accountable for fulfilling those expectations.

- Leaders need to ensure all employees understand the link between their written performance goals and clearly stated behavioral expectations.
- When leaders clarify what employees will be held accountable for in terms of performance goals and behavioral expectations, employees can hold themselves personally accountable. When employees do so, they should be rewarded.

In the next chapter, we will explore the next of the five elements of engagement: The Element of Connectedness.

Chapter 5

The Element of Connectedness

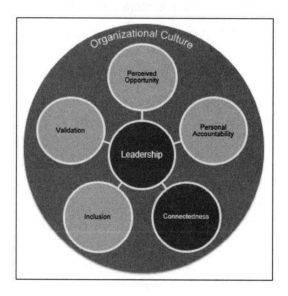

Premise: Engagement occurs when employees feel connected with each other, focus on mutual interests, and share responsibility.

F eeling connected, experiencing the support of others, and sharing responsibility for outcomes all lead to reengagement. Unfortunately, staying connected is a challenge for a variety of reasons. We again return to Avcor as an illustration of what can happen.

Avcor was organized as two primary functional units. One segment focused on the development and marketing of generic applications used by the majority of its customers who had similar software needs. The other functional unit served customers who needed customized applications that provided solutions for unique situations. Although the generic product group focused primarily on new products, the group that focused on customization served more as consultants to customers. A senior vice president who reported directly to the company president headed each group. Nancy did her best to acknowledge the importance of both divisions and expected a high level of collaboration and exchange of information between them. Her team, comprised of the two business units as well as professional support groups such as finance, legal, and human resources, met often and spent the majority of time focused on leading the business.

When the new president took Nancy's place, the harmony among business unit leaders began to erode. Even before the change of leadership, the two senior vice presidents thought of themselves as competitors. Many of their customers could either chose to use generic applications or custom applications; therefore, each Avcor group worked hard to get the common customer to select its product or service. With the new president's focus on reductions and cost savings, the two vice presidents also found themselves competing for operating funds, new hires, and investment dollars.

The president made it known that he felt the era of generic product would soon begin to decline and felt the future was in customized services. The head of the customization group quickly became the president's confidant and used his position to further his cause at the cost of the generic group. Both senior vice presidents, having their own groups' best interest in mind, began to put up barriers. Information was no longer shared. Trust and positive intentions were questioned. Neither group knew what the other group was doing. The president looked at what was occurring as healthy competition, but in reality it had split the organization, reduced productivity, and resulted in key employees especially in the generic group looking elsewhere for employment. Avcor had lost its feeling of connectedness.

The Differentiated Organization

Young, successful companies often have a natural sense of connectedness—referred to as a "small company or family like culture"—one in which everyone knows everyone else, communication happens face-to-face, and members huddle informally rather than having scheduled meetings. In these organizations, employees feel energized and committed to each other, often with a strong feeling of support and camaraderie. In addition, these types of organizations can easily hire individuals who share the same values and beliefs. However, as an organization grows, maintaining a true sense of connectedness becomes a challenge. What happens?

Geographical disconnection

We're currently working with an organization that's experiencing healthy growth. As a result, it's disconnecting, a concern to all involved. In a two-year span, the company has tripled the number of its employees. One consequence is that the company has outgrown its ability to keep everyone in one building and has since moved a large group of employees to a second location approximately fifteen miles from where they once all worked together. Although the two buildings are still relatively close, many of the employees now feel like there are two different organizations. Management is amazed at how this move has disconnected the organization. Perhaps the biggest sense of loss in separating employees is the loss of personal interaction. Often the tone of an organization is set by little things: hallway conversations, just-in-time meetings to resolve an issue, or time spent playing cards during lunch in the cafeteria.

In addition, as a means of expanding its geographical presence and services, this company has been buying smaller businesses with ten to twenty employees in various out-of-state locations. These small businesses have their own ways of doing business and continue to identify with their well-established brands rather than adopt the name of the larger firm. Consequently, their connection and identity is with their local firm, which can create an us-versus-them mentality. Employees at remote locations may also feel that they don't get the support they need of feel included in many of the daily forms of information sharing. Therefore, it's easy to feel disconnected geographically.

Organizational segmentation

Organizational segmentation can also occur when differentiation drives how leaders think and act much like in the Avcor case study. As soon as an organization separates business units or creates formal departments—finance, IT, human resources, and operations—differentiation begins to occur: "You handle this. I'll handle that" and, "You have responsibility for custom applications. I have responsibility for generic applications." In this scenario, employees become more specialized.

123

Functions grow increasingly different from one another. Identity is with their specific functional unit, not with other business units. Employees can easily lose their sense of being in the same boat sailing in the same direction. Leaders begin to believe their primary responsibility is to represent their part of the business rather than the business as a whole. Although differentiation is critical to the efficiency and ultimately the success of a business, employees can easily get stuck in it. Here we illustrate what can occur:

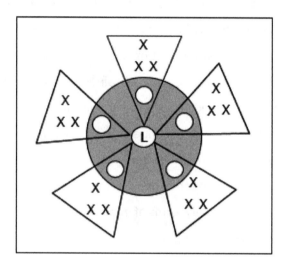

Assume this illustration is a meeting of the president and his or her team of direct reports in a midsize organization. The L in the center circle represents the leader. The pie slices represent various disciplines or functions. The small circles represent the heads of various disciplines that make up the leadership team. The Xs represent those employees reporting to the heads of various disciplines.

Functional segmentation occurs if the various leaders (HR, marketing, finance, manufacturing, and so forth) around the table believe they are there to primarily represent their slice of the business. Their mindset is one of advocating for their function's needs or defending what they do or why they do it. This creates what Barry Oshry in his book, *Seeing Systems: Unlocking the Mysteries of Organizational Life,* refers to as "spacial blindness," seeing the part without the whole. If that's the case, where segmentation drives certain behaviors, there will be little opportunity to be a high-performing team or an aligned leadership.

If differentiation drives much of the team's behavior, some of the following symptoms are likely part of the dynamics:

- Only the leader, which is the key point, owns the whole circle (the business) and often spends significant energy working one-on-one with various functional leaders concerned only with their part of the circle (their function).
- Each functional leader will try to make his or her own deals with the leader believing that's the best strategy for getting what he or she wants. The leader spends an inordinate amount of time trying to reconcile perceived functional differences and his or her particular needs.
- Goals and planning are built within functions or disciplines, not between them. Although a strategic plan may exist that speaks to the organization's future plans, most of the energy is spent within disciplines where they create a strategy specific to what the function wants to accomplish.

For example, one of our clients is an organization that spans the United States. In order to function more effectively, the organization has created geographic regions: Northeast, Southeast, Central, and Western. A chief operating officer who is responsible for the success of his or her own region leads each region who has a significant amount of autonomy, which consequently means the goals, practices, processes, and focus can be significantly different from region to region, and which can result in what is referred to as "a company of little arrows" illustrated here:

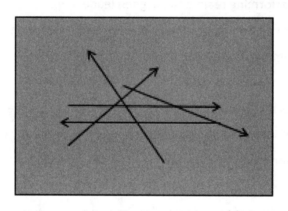

Each little arrow represents one of the regions or a professional service group (marketing, HR, legal, finance). Within each arrow, everything looks aligned. Each arrow builds a business plan, setting a direction. However, if you look at the organization as a whole, the arrows aren't aligned with each other. Consequently, little connectedness is evident, and each region interprets strategy to its own liking. The interpretations are often different from each other, and those employees at lower levels within the organization who become confused by the inconsistencies feel the consequences. When an opportunity to work together across arrows occurs, developing a strategy can become difficult because the organization acts like a confederacy of small companies rather than a unified whole.

Symptoms of differentiation

Although this company is experiencing strong growth, a significant amount of organizational energy is spent internally solving the many issues that result from being seen as a confederacy. When projects cross boundaries, a lot of energy goes into figuring out how to split the project and the costs. When corporate wants to introduce a solution to address a problem or opportunity that crosses boundaries, resistance occurs because regions do things differently. From all appearances they may believe what they're doing is equal to or better than what corporate is introducing. Implementing broad initiatives is often seen as an intrusion on the region's autonomy.

Let's continue with a list of differentiated symptoms:

- **Functional or role boundaries are protected.** Although the organization probably pays lip service to collaborative efforts, the different regions or functions spend energy protecting their borders instead of being partners with each other, and they feel they need to defend themselves from each other.
- **Entrenched views of what's important to the business emerge based on each region or function's mindset.** Finance sees the corporate world through a different lens than HR or sales sees the same world. Finance focuses on finance issues: profit, EBIT, and costs. HR focuses on people issues: training, succession planning, talent, and leadership. The sales organization focuses

127

on the customer, presentations, and marketing. As a result, they disconnect from each other, making collaboration more difficult.

- **People within one discipline aren't made aware of what's going on in other disciplines.** Because of differentiation, a lot of communication challenges arise. Within a given function, information sharing occurs at a relatively high level whereas between functions leaders and employees direct little energy toward sharing information. Consequently, ways to support and stand in for each other are missing.

- **Information becomes power.** A group or function guards communication and makes decisions regarding what information to share and how to share it. Decisions are made regarding what and how information should be shared. What does corporate need to know? What do other disciplines need to know? The lack of information sharing results in misunderstandings. Corporate leaders are often surprised when a crisis occurs in a region because they had been kept in the dark until the crisis occurred.

- **Groups are unnecessarily seen as competing with each other, thus creating a win-lose feeling.** In some situations, one group is doing better than another. Corporate recognizes the successful group for its efforts. On the other hand, if a group is struggling, corporate often tends to be critical of that group rather than be supportive.

- **Trust and positive intent are often questioned.** If differentiation is strong and trust among disciplines is low, interactions are tense with the disciplines spending energy to maintain relationships rather than grow them.

> **Given what we have just shared about differentiation, what is symptomatic of your organization? What is the impact on teams in your organization?**

The various ways differentiation disconnects the organization can take the joy out of being a team member, create a sense of disinterest, and lead to a culture where employees put in their time but no longer their energy.

Disconnected beliefs and values

When an organization is small, hiring individuals who share similar values and beliefs is one of the gates to employment. Employees not only share what they do, but more importantly they share why they do it—a common purpose. According to Simon Sinek in his book, *Start with Why: How Great Leaders Inspire Others,* as the organization grows, a split begins to occur when the organization begins hiring for positions and not beliefs. How a candidate looks on paper is the criterion for hiring rather than shared values or beliefs. These new hires have good technical skills and know what their job is, but they may lack the organization's why—why do we do what we do and what we believe and value. When this begins to occur, stress goes up, passion goes down, you hear the statement, "It's not like it used to be," and the organization loses connectedness because its cause or purpose can be lost.

In summary, staying connected is a significant challenge as organizations grow. In today's modern work practices, even small business can experience disconnection. The more disconnected the organization becomes, the more likely the employees are to unplug or disengage. Our research indicated that employees want to be connected, they want to feel supported by others, and they want to collaborate and feel a sense of sharing responsibility. Part of reengagement is establishing a culture of connectedness. The next section will focus on how you accomplish that.

Creating Connectedness

Companies must remake themselves into places of engagement where people are committed to one another and to their enterprise. The best way to do so is by enhancing the element of connectedness. Each of the core reasons organizations disconnect has a series of ways to reconnect.

Making connections

The following are considerations for addressing the various ways organizations disconnect. Some of these suggestions are clear and we only summarize them, whereas we address others in more detail.

> One of the key responsibilities of leadership is to make connections, making sure the right people are connected to each other.

This can apply to employees separated by distance and also by employees separated by function.

The following model will help you look at your own situation and provide insight into how you can enhance connectedness:

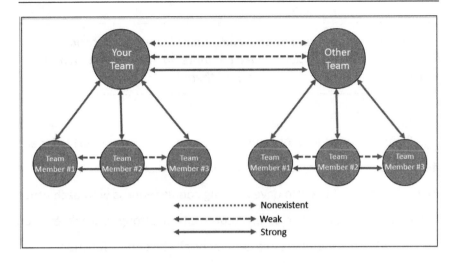

This model represents the level of connectedness within and across functions or locations. The top circles represent a leader and his or her team, function, or location. In this illustration we will use different functions as an example. The three circles at the bottom show three team members in each of two functions. Assume they represent direct reports.

The lines demonstrate the level of connectedness among the individuals in this illustration. The level of connectedness can range from nonexistent to weak to strong in an organization's culture. The level of connectedness between one functional leader and various colleagues often cover all three options. The functional leader may have some strong connections with certain other leaders, and weaker or nonexistent connections with other leaders. For example, a strong connection would probably exist between the marketing team and the sales team. The connection might be weaker between the marketing team and IT because they don't spend as much time working with each other.

> *Think of the other functional heads, team leaders, or location heads who are your peers. Take a minute and assess how strong your connectedness is with each of them.*

Ideally, a strong level of connectedness exists between the leader and team members or direct reports on different teams, functions, or locations. Team members also have a strong connectedness with each other. However, varying levels of connectedness, from strong to weak, exist on teams with team members in a geographically dispersed function.

> *Think of the employees within your function, location, or team. Take a minute and assess how strong your connectedness is with each employee and with each other.*

Connectedness in many organizations is often weaker between one leader's function, location, or team members and the members of other functions, locations, or teams. The leaders from the different function, location, or team may be connected, but their employees aren't. This would be true of an organization if the following scenario occurs.

> *If one of your team members has a problem with a member of another team, where does he or she go for resolution?*

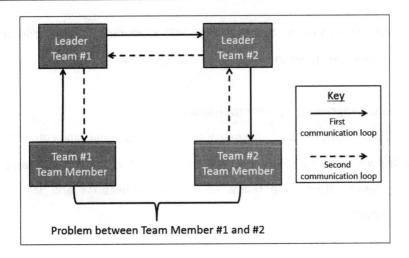

Problem between Team Member #1 and #2

Again, using functional segmentation as our example, assume an employee of yours has a problem with an employee in another department. The employee believes you have the best opportunity to solve the problem. If the connection you have with the other department leader is positive, that leader can help by going to her other employee and asking for some form of resolution. That leader then communicates the resolution back to you, and you take it to your employee. If resolution doesn't occur, the problem can go back and forth between you and the other leader, taking a considerable amount of time and energy.

A key role of leadership is to make the right connections—putting the right employees together with each other to enhance their productivity and engagement. In the previous example, if the employees from the two departments had been connected, had built a strong working relationship, and therefore had dealt with each other, they could have resolved the issue without involving leadership, thus saving much energy and time.

The first step in reconnecting when a geographical or functional separation exists is to make connections among employees who are likely to interact with each other over time. After connections are made, the employees can apply some of the following additional suggestions.

Making geographic segmentation work

Sarah Kelly, head of Pharmaceutical Sciences Small Molecule, Pfizer Worldwide Research and Development, provided us with a great example of ensuring structuring teams to enable connections and fostering collaboration:

> In the pharmaceutical industry, work is typically done on new products in the research arm of the business, and as the products move forward into development and successfully perform in clinical trials, they will be scaled up and commercialized in the manufacturing division. There are many models of how this works but one top-performing example is at Pfizer. Joint teams are formed with representatives across both divisions as a product enters Phase 2 to Phase 3 clinical trials (three to five years from launch). These teams work together across widely different time zones and geographies to engage in what is called 'co-development' of a new drug. The teams are governed by one body with representatives and decision makers from research, quality, regulatory, and manufacturing all aligned to a common deliverable. As technical issues arise, they are jointly solved. This model has been in place for decades. At its core are strong relationships and collaboration that must come together to jointly deliver a product.

Familiarity

A common form of geographic inclusion is familiarity.

> The more familiar employees are with each other, even when geographically distanced from each other, the more likely they are to communicate and collaborate.

On the other hand, if employees know each other only by name or reputation, the likelihood that connectedness will occur is low. To establish *familiarity*, have employees who need to connect meet each other face-to-face with the purpose of getting to know each other and plan the best ways to communicate. If getting together in person isn't easy, then have them spend some time on videoconference or on the phone learning about each other and establishing ways to stay connected.

Cross-pollination

In our earlier example of geographical disconnection where the company as a means of expanding its geographical presence and services acquired smaller businesses with ten to twenty employees in various out-of-state locations, cross pollination was a key strategy. Offering employees the opportunity to relocate to one of the smaller geographic locations or allowing an employee from one of the smaller locations to spend a period of time at the company's headquarters proved beneficial. Doing so allowed employees to become more familiar with each other, which became a strong example of mutual influence. Both parties could learn different practices from each other, learn how small or large companies operate, share values and beliefs, and become familiar with each other.

Virtual teams

If employees are geographically segmented and serve a similar service or function as those employees in other locations, having them identify as a virtual team helps connectedness. A virtual team (also known as a *geographically dispersed team, distributed team,* or *remote team*) is a group of individuals who work across time, space, and organizational boundaries with links strengthened by forms of communication technology. Familiarity is critical to starting this connectedness strategy. An initial meeting, face-to-face if possible, allows team members to get to know each other and what they believe they add to the team. This chartering session allows the team to set expectations, develop a common purpose, create a set of guidelines for team interaction, and frame the work in which the team needs to focus. Giving employees the opportunity to get to know each other and having them participate in creating a team identity lays the foundation for operating as a virtual team.

> Two additional ingredients for the successful use of virtual teams is the strength of who is leading the process and strong technology that allows for easy visual and audible interactions.

Functional Segmentation

The second reason why organizations disconnect is functional segmentation. The company's functions differentiate themselves from each other and can develop a silo mentality, put up barriers to collaboration, and advocate and defend for their part of the whole. In order to create connectedness, the company has to cover this differentiation. The following are practices that contribute to doing so:

De-differentiation

De-differentiation is the act of setting aside differentiated thinking that segments a group—many hats—and wearing what is referred to as "one hat."

In order to successfully connect, leaders or employees representing different functions must learn to take off their individual hats (their functional identities) and put on one hat that speaks to the whole that unites them all. For example, if a senior team consisting of members of HR, finance, business development, and manufacturing is together, "one hat" implies everyone temporarily sets aside the belief they are there to represent their function and put on a hat that changes their mindset to focus on what it means to be responsible for the whole—the business. The team must accept this identity to truly feel connected. There are certainly times when arguing for and defending one's functional piece of the pie is appropriate, but the team needs to be focused a majority of time on one level above that from which the team normally thinks and acts. The "one hat" may read "leadership" or the name of the organization and implies functional leaders taken collective responsibility for leading the organization. This applies within a function as well. How does the team look at itself as leading the function?

A friend of ours from Millikan, the large textile company centered in Spartanburg, South Carolina, referred to de-differentiation as the "law of the higher helicopter." He drew us a picture of helicopters close to the ground:

The closer the helicopter flies to the ground, the more limited the pilot is in what he or she sees. Each pilot sees a different picture of the terrain. Consequently, the pilot has more difficulty both understanding what other pilots see and/or caring only for the part he or she sees. When different functions are trying to connect, the key is to fly higher. When doing so, the landscape takes on a different perspective and all the pilots see the whole rather than just their part.

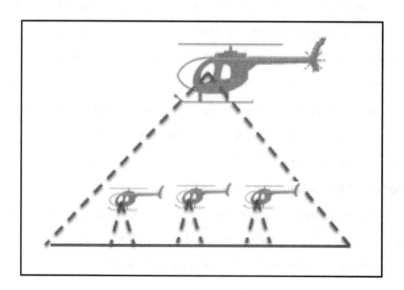

Some years ago, Skanska USA Building had a leadership team made up of regional COOs and a professional service groups (legal, finance, project controls, and more). Everyone was segmented along these lines

and flying low level helicopters. They were differentiated, and some of the members described them as dysfunctional. A change of leadership brought Bill Flemming into the team as president, and one of his first acts was to gather his senior leadership team and create a set of values, one of which was referred to as "one hat." The definition of this value was: "We will spend our time together focused on how to lead the organization rather than on individual agendas or simple information sharing."

Rather than being the leader, he created a shared responsibility team. Now everyone spends a majority of their time together focused on the business and on what it means to lead as a team.

Developing a Collaborative Mindset

A second way to enhance connectedness is creating a collaborative mindset within the culture.

As collaboration at all levels increases, so does connectedness, and engagement increases.

High-performing organizations will often point to their success by talking about their collaborative culture and the impact it has on productivity. There are two contributing factors to accomplishing a collaborative culture:

- The first is the feeling of working with colleagues who trust and support each other and who demonstrate interest in not only their own success, but also in the success of their colleagues.

Sustaining engagement is difficult when employees feel disconnected to their peers and support for each other isn't evident.

- The second is to operate with a collaborative mindset, the process of integrating different functions or individual perspectives
to accomplish a common outcome.

Three mindsets can exist within organizations. They are referred to as
competitive, compromise, and collaborative.

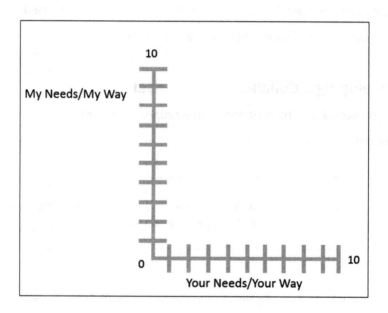

The mindsets model looks at two dimensions:

- My needs/my way
- Your needs/your way

A 0 on the scale implies the person doesn't get his or her way, whereas a 10 implies the person gets his or her way. Assume you're sitting down with the heads of all other functions. The president has just announced an increased budget for hiring four new full-time employees. Although this news is good, in reality, it's insufficient to fill the hiring needs of the departments making requests. Each function put in a request for four new employees, so as one of the leaders, you all have to reach an agreement as to how many hires you each get.

Because each leader could use all four hires, human nature is to argue for your needs or referring to the model, get as close to 10 as you can, which means your needs or wants are satisfied, but all the leaders around the table want to win. Everyone hates to feel that they've lost.

You'll probably work hard to make sure the other leaders understand why the resources should go to your department and at the same time they'll likely argue that they need the resources for their needs. And if you get the resources and the other departments don't, you hope they won't get angry or upset. Other leaders hold the same beliefs. These three scenarios that represent the different mindsets encountered in organizations can play out of this situation:

Competitive

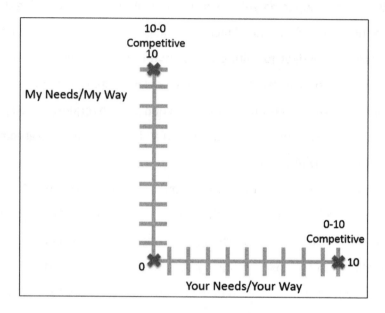

This competitive scenario would play out as 10–0 on the matrix. One function gets its resources and you don't. This scenario is referred to as win-lose. If I win, you lose, so I view that as 10–0 in my favor. If you win, I lose, then I view that as 0–10 in your favor. When you hold this mindset, you tend to advocate for your needs. The other departments will advocate for its needs. You may find yourself arguing over who needs the resources the most and who benefited most the last time resources were available. You even possibly accuse whom you're arguing with that they're being selfish or unfair. The discussion may escalate, and you can end up upset with the other functional leaders. If you get all the resources and the other parties don't, then you're happy and the other leaders are unhappy. This leaves the group disconnected.

> *Do you find elements of a 10–0 mindset in your culture? Is there a lot of competition between individuals and/or groups? Are individuals rewarded for winning?*

Compromise

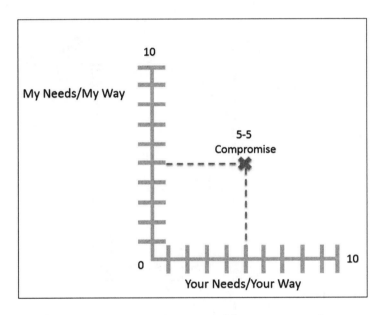

There is an easier way to tackle the resource question. Forget the various reasons the functions give for needing the resources; simply give each function one of the new hires. With this 5–5 compromise scenario, "I get part of my way and you get part of your way." No one really wins, but on the hand, no one really loses. This may leave both parties feeling that that's the best resolution, but is it? The parties at least avoided conflict, and no function felt like it lost. Too often, compromise is used to avoid conflict rather than to clearly address the question: "Who needs the resources most?"

Does your organization tend to use compromise as a means to settle difficult situations? Does compromising best serve the needs of the organization? Does it serve you?

Collaborative

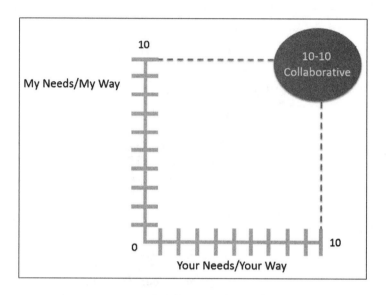

The third option is collaborative. Assume when the discussion of resources begins, the focus is on the following questions: "What are we all interested in solving?" and "What is in the best interest of the larger organization?" The focus is on the various parties collaborating to come up with the best solution, which is referred to as 10–10, or win-win. Collaboration is occurring because the leaders are focused on the organization's needs rather than on their own needs. They used the organization rather than their own situations to determine what was best. For a collaborative mindset to exist, one key ingredient must always be present: mutual interest. What do both parties want? If in this scenario, both parties agree what they want is what is best for the long-term health and stability of the organization, mutual interest is established. When the interest is focused on the organization's long-term needs, it becomes the criteria for slotting jobs. The leaders may leave feeling they helped solve an organizational problem that in the long term will benefit everyone. Doing so creates a high degree of connectedness.

> For a collaborative mindset to exist, one key ingredient must always be present: mutual interest.

In the example that Sarah Kelly from Pfizer Worldwide Research and Development provided, she emphasized not only do leaders need to structure ways for dispersed teams to get together, but more importantly, leaders need to be aligned around a common deliverable, which requires strong relationships and a mindset of collaboration.

> *Is your culture set up for looking at mutual interest? Do individuals tend to ask the question: "What is best for the organization?" Are individuals rewarded for finding the best solution?*

Mutual Influence and a Collaborative Culture

In chapter two, we introduced the concept of mutual influence relationships, using the following definition: "Mutual influence means that each person can influence the ideas and behaviors of others. A mutual influence relationship is an open working relationship in which both individuals are free to speak freely, challenge each other, and hear and accept what the other offers."

When teams operate with a collaborative mindset, all members need to be clear about the team goal that they're trying to achieve together, connect to the goal, and influence each other on how best to accomplish it. In a collaborative culture, members can feel free to influence others, but they must also have the skills to do so. As a leader, you play the most critical role in creating a collaborative culture first by practicing mutual influence skills and also by creating the expectations that everyone has the skills to practice mutual influence. Mutual influence involves being able to:

- Be clear and direct about what you think is important/what you need to do your part.
- Listen to what the other person thinks is important and needs.
- Disagree on the means of achieving the goal without blaming or judging.
- Accept legitimacy of others wanting different things/having different viewpoints.
- Engage in joint problem solving to achieve mutual goals.

In order to influence other, individuals must communicate directly and openly with the intent of accomplishing a shared purpose. Three skill sets help people connect with each other and collaborate to create something of value:

Mutual Influence Skills

- Listen to learn
- Express to explore
- Integrate to innovate

Listen to learn

In a collaborative culture, the ideal is to listen for the benefit of understanding the ideas and assumptions of others in order to create solutions together. Depending on the mindset of the individual—competitive, compromise, or collaborative—people tend to listen for different reasons. In a mindset of competition, people often listen to arm themselves to win a point or refute what the other person has said. In a mindset of compromise, the intent is to create harmony and make others feel good. However, in a collaborative mindset, the intent is to learn about differences and draw from them in creating the best solutions.

Listen to learn means listening for the interests and perspectives others may be providing. In order to build on differences to create great solutions, it's necessary to surface the differences. Listening helps you hear and understand the meaning in different viewpoints. Here are the specific skills needed to do this:

- Seek different points of view.
- Probe to clarify perspectives, assumptions, and interests.
- Check interpretations to ensure understanding.

Use *reflective listening* to focus on the meaning of what the person is saying:

- Listen for the essence of what the person is saying.
- Listen for the interests behind the message.
- Summarize what you've heard.

Use *investigative listening* to think about what questions you might ask to:

- Clarify the message.
- Complete your understanding.
- Test your interpretations.

By applying this skill set, you focus on others' point of view with the intention of learning. When others are understood, they're open to the influence of others.

Express to explore

While some individuals are listening, others are expressing their ideas. Often people express themselves to advocate their ideas or to persuade others. As with this skill set, depending on the individual's mindset—competitive, compromise, or collaborative—people tend to express themselves for different reasons. In the mindset of competition, the intent is to win and have one's own ideas prevail. In a mindset of com-promise, the intent is to avoid offending anyone and to make everyone feel good. However, in a collaborative mindset, the intent is to contribute to accomplishing a shared purpose.

Express to explore means expressing your ideas for the benefit of examining them and connecting to other ideas. It's important to test your ideas and express them in a way that invites examination and suggestions for improvement. How you communicate your ideas will determine whether they'll be considered part of the solution. These specific skills will help you accomplish it:

- Offer ideas and opinions for group examination.
- Invite questions to test everyone's assumptions.

When initiating an idea,

- Convey the idea openly.
- Explain assumptions or reasoning.
- Invite support and criticism.
- Ask for suggestions.

When responding to an idea,

- Ask for clarification.
- Offer support and alternative viewpoints.
- Offer suggestions for improvement or enhancement.
- Ask for different perspectives.

This skill set allows you to put an idea forward without having to be sure or right about it. You can introduce ideas without an attachment to them, that is, in a way that's neutral that separates you from your ideas, so people are encouraged to build upon them, challenge them, or accept them.

Integrate to innovate

Behaviors alone won't lead to collaboration. What's also important is the intention behind the behavior. Others will only be influenced by your ideas if they believe you intend to help create a better solution. Better solutions that serve multiple interests and truly solve the problem are created when you integrate diverse ideas. These specific skills will help you accomplish it:

- Articulate the problem you're trying to solve or the outcome you're trying to achieve. State the problem or desired outcome in a simple sentence. Agree the stated problem is what you want to solve.
- Prioritize interests of key stakeholders by identifying them and their primary interests. Challenge assumptions about each interest and weigh the relative importance of each interest.
- Consider options that meet multiple interests. Brainstorm ways to include priority interests in possible solutions that will achieve the desired outcome. Try applying a both/and approach, or asking "What if. . .?"

- Combine diverse ideas into an innovate solution. Configure different options and evaluate the likely results. Modify the solution to achieve the desired outcome.

In applying this skill set, focus on incorporating all viewpoints to create the best solution. After you have listened to their perspectives, understood their concerns, examined all ideas, challenged each other's assumptions, and created possible options, you can determine the best solution for achieving the desired outcome.

Summary of mutual influence and collaboration

By listening to learn, you appreciate what others have to say and attempt to sincerely understand them, so they may influence you and you may build on their ideas.

By expressing to explore, you consider what's required and then contribute your ideas, influencing others to consider them and build on them as part of a solution.

By integrating to innovate, you incorporate the best ideas to co-create a solution that achieves the outcome in a way that serves stakeholder interests.

The Use of Teams

The third way to create connectedness is the strategic use of teams. The differentiation that separates members of leadership or cross-functional teams needs to be overcome. If not, leaders or employees enter the team space prepared to defend and advocate for their slice of the pie, which creates the office politics, the infighting, and the competition that kills productivity and diminishes engagement. What are referred to as *silos,* segmented teams create a significant energy drain because they set up battles with employees who should be their teammates.

To counter this, a team must achieve alignment by de-differentiating, wearing one hat, and creating a "big arrow." To do so, a team uses a chartering process that aligns the smaller arrows (discussed earlier) and creates strategic unity.

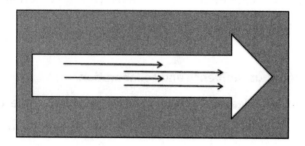

The intent of the big arrow isn't to decrease the identity of individual functions; it's to align them. In doing so, they share a higher level of responsibility for the whole and feel a higher level of connectedness.

What would characterize a connected team? Following are the benchmarks for a high-performing team:

- The team members stand together. They demonstrate consistent actions and an aligned voice.
- Together, the team spends time on the balcony. The team steps back, observes the fray, and interprets the needs of the whole function or organization.

- The team members trust each other's intent and competency and have a way to safely confront and challenge each other. Strong transparency is evident.
- The team members demonstrate a collaborative mindset.
- The team members really listen and learn from each other. Information sharing occurs naturally.
- The team members practice collective decision-making around key imperatives.
- The team members discipline themselves to execute.
- The team members practice mutual influence.
- The team members adhere to a set of values (terms of engagement) upon which they consistently act.
- The team members share responsibility: "If we succeed, we all succeed; if we fail, we all fail."
- The team members think of themselves as being in the energy business.
- They create a single identity: the big arrow.

How do your teams measure up to these attributes?

Real-time application: Chartering

The purpose of this activity is to introduce a process that builds the big arrow and increases connectedness within work groups or teams. Part of your job as a leader is to build connectedness with those you lead, which may be your work team or your managers. The process is called *chartering.*

Following are the steps for the leader:

- Identify your team and schedule a half to a full day to meet together.
- Create a set of worksheets that reflect the questions the team needs to answer.
- Engage your team in answering the following questions:
  - ✓ Whom do we serve? Who is our primary constituency and what do they require of us?
  - ✓ Are there critical interfaces necessary to succeed?
  - ✓ What is our desired outcome or purpose? How will the outcome benefit all team members and our constituents?
  - ✓ What will success look like?
  - ✓ What procedures will we need to put in place?
  - ✓ What roles will individuals play?
  - ✓ How will we relate to each other?
- Use the results to guide the team moving forward.

The primary purpose is to create strategic unity. You align the team members regarding who they want to be and what they want to accomplish. A by-product is unity—strong connectedness and shared responsibility. As a result, teams de-differentiate, align, and connect with each other. As collaboration at all levels increases, so does connectedness and thus, engagement.

Values and beliefs

A third way organizations disconnect is with their values and beliefs.

What are values?

From an organizational perspective, *values* serve as the basis for what an organization expects of its employees. Here are some examples:

- **Collaboration:** We as an organization are committed to working with each other and to encourage our employees to do the same.
- **Commitment:** We'll keep the promises, large and small, that we make to each other.
- **Learning:** We'll share information, discoveries, insights, and mistakes, when the knowledge can benefit the rest of the organization.

When an organization states values like these, the organization is also communicating an expectation to employees to behave accordingly.

At the same time, each employee has his or her values. These values serve as the basis of one's behavior and motivation. Values essentially describe what a person desires or seeks to achieve. If a person says he or she values competitiveness, this will likely be visible in their behavior. When organizations are small, they often emphasize whether the values of employment candidate are similar to those of the organization. As noted earlier, as an organization grows, it places more emphasis on resumes, and it may not note value differences. If the organization values collaboration, but an employee values competitiveness, there is a disconnection.

What are beliefs?

Beliefs are judgments people make about themselves and the world around them. They shape a person's map of reality. They're usually generalizations, and a typical belief may be "Profits are all that are important to our company." Sometimes beliefs become strongly entrenched or emotional. If the organization strives for profits but emphasizes the core belief that good customer service leads to a sustainable business, there may easily be a disconnect. The employee demonstrates discontent because he or she doesn't believe the organization has the customer in mind as he or she believes they should.

As the values and beliefs of employees disconnect from the organization's values and beliefs, several possible consequences can occur: turnover increases, discontent increases, tension increases, passion decreases, and so on.

The following are a few suggestions to keep the organization and its employees connected regarding values and beliefs:

Interview process

If values are the basis of one's behavior and describe what a person desires or seeks to achieve, they should reveal themselves during the interview process. Listen for them. You can also ask any of these certain questions that may help provide a sense of what the candidate values and believes:

- Why do you want this job?
- What are your criteria or measures for deciding if this job is right for you?

- What value do you bring to the organization or, in simpler terms, "what am I buying?"
- How do you see yourself contributing to the organization?
- When you are at your best, what are you doing?
- In your last job, what part of your work gave you energy?
- If you were interviewing me, what questions would you ask?

Onboarding

If you have hired someone you feel is a strong candidate, then onboarding is the next natural place to connect the new employee to the organization's values and beliefs. *Onboarding,* also known as *organizational socialization,* is the process by which new hires get adjusted to the social and performance aspects of their job. This can involve holding introductory meetings, orienting them to their new role and related expectations, connecting them to existing employees, completing paperwork, and in some cases understanding the culture in which they're being integrated.

We recommend making the organizations values (how you expect employees to behave) and beliefs explicit to your new employees. Make sure they understand what they are and the consequences of not adhering to them.

For all employees, make the values and beliefs visible to them, continue to remind them what the organization's values are, and provide examples of how those values are demonstrated.

Shared purpose: Create the why

Have you ever been part of a social gathering and someone asked you, "What do you do for a living?"

We have and we respond by sharing aspects of our work.

How many times have you been asked this same question?

Likewise, in organizations the focus is often on what and how the work is done and not on why the work is done. Understanding the why of what employees do as employees and understanding the why the organization does what it does is the connecting belief element that brings employees a clear sense of what the purpose of their work is. As stated in chapter three, Simon Sinek, author of *Start with Why: How Great Leaders Inspire Others to Take Action*, believes that inspired leaders work from the inside out. They start with the why—why they do what they do—move to the how—how the work will get done—and lastly, finish with the what—what is the product, much like the essence-based leadership required to reengage the organization, inside out rather than outside in.

Make sure employees are clear on their why. The key isn't to hire based on a resume alone but to hire people who believe what you believe. Help them identify what their purpose is and what the organization's purpose is. In doing so, you connect the employees' values and beliefs to the organization's values and beliefs.

Chapter Summary

Engagement can't be sustained if employees don't have a sense of trust and support from their colleagues. Unfortunately, segmenting the organization geographically or functionally into divisions, departments, and roles, disconnects the organization from organizational values and beliefs. The consequence is that employees feel disconnected from each other and from the organization as a whole.

Leaders need to facilitate a high level of connectedness geographically, functionally, and through values and beliefs. This chapter provided both an understanding of why organizations disconnect and provided a variety of ways to reconnect.

In our next chapter, we will explore the next of the five elements of engagement: The Element of Inclusion.

Chapter 6

The Element of Inclusion

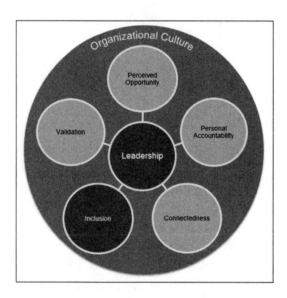

Premise: **Engagement happens when employees are well informed and involved and have an opportunity to openly express their thoughts and feelings. Simply stated, people want to feel like they're in on things.**

In this chapter we'll return to Avcor as a way to better understand what can quiet an organization. We'll identify behaviors that suppress communication and introduce the importance of trust. We'll shift focus and introduce a variety of inclusion elements that help reengage employees.

One of the observable characteristics of an organization that has unplugged is the noise level goes way down. *Noise* means the general sound of employees talking, interacting, and enjoying each other. What creates this condition? In Avcor's situation, Nancy was transparent regarding all aspects of the business. She frequently led town hall meetings where she detailed the organization's health. She talked openly about her vision for the organization and her excitement about future opportunities. She was always open to questions and encouraged others to share their thoughts and ideas. Nancy had created an open environment where employees felt included. Employees could be candid with her regarding problems, and she welcomed feedback on how she was doing.

During the acquisition Nancy did her best to keep everyone informed regarding the many changes. What surprised many employees was the lack of information that the acquiring committee provided. The new leaders made little effort to share their vision for the future, the way Avcor fit in to their plans, or their purpose and mission. Some employees went to the acquiring company's annual report in order to better understand for whom they worked.

After Nancy resigned and the financial executive took over the leadership role of Avcor, he initially held a company-wide meeting to introduce himself and share his excitement about leading the organization into the future. However, following this initial display, his visibility and frequency of communicating began to decline. Often no one heard anything from him for extensive periods of time. When the infrequent company-wide meeting was held, it focused almost entirely on the company's state from a financial perspective. He tended to point out problems rather than opportunities. During these meetings, he gave employees few opportunities to ask questions, and he never asked for their insights.

On more than one occasion, employees did ask questions and received vague answers. Employees felt he withheld information. They knew something important was going on, but because they didn't know the full story, they naturally overinterpreted any shard of information they did get their hands on. In other situations, the leader reacted to questions or comments by getting angry or defensive and in so doing, discounted both the employee asking the question and the importance of asking questions. Soon, no one bothered to ask questions, no one offered input, and fewer and fewer employees showed up for his informational meetings. Consequently, the leader stopped having meetings because from his perception, employees didn't care. The organization had become quiet.

Sharing information, seeking employee input, and listening are some of the most powerful tools of engagement a leader has. When a leader doesn't share information, when a leader is described as not listening, and when employees feel they have no venue to share feelings and thoughts, engagement decreases.

Consider the following questions when thinking about your organization:

- Have you been part of a work culture when there was/is an absence of information being exchanged? What happened?
- What do you view are the greatest communication problems or challenges you encounter in your organization?

- Regarding communication practices, what do you believe leadership in your organization does well?
- Technology has made communicating easier, but has it made it more effective in your organization?

On a scale of 1 to 5, with 1 being needs work to 5 being excellent, how would you rate your own communication effectiveness?

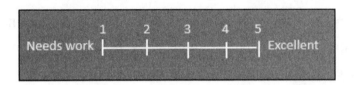

What Quiets the Organization?

There are many factors that can lead to an organization going quiet. The following describe what we have found to be particularly important when trying to understand what can quiet the organization.

Willingness

Most leaders are all well informed regarding the practices of inclusion listening, asking, sharing, providing feedback, involving others, and using verbal and written communications. These all represent *abilities,* or the ability to communicate. On the other hand, is the issue of willingness. *Willingness* is the effort, time, or energy you put into the communication encounter.

In group sessions, Steve often asks participants the following questions:

- I'll give you a thousand dollars to listen to me. Could you do it?
- I'll give you a thousand dollars to share information with me. Could you do it?
- I'll give you a thousand dollars to share your feelings. Could you do it?

As you would expect, every participant says yes. So what does this answer imply? It implies people have the ability to practice forms of inclusion. However, what's often missing is the willingness to give the communication encounter one's attention, energy, or time. If employees conclude that leadership isn't giving the appropriate time, energy, and attention to communicating information and including them, engagement decreases.

The perception of importance

The importance that leaders place on communicating is why they give time, energy, and attention to a communication event or fail to do.

In other words, importance is about the priority placed on any information transaction. The higher the importance, the more willing leaders are to apply their communication abilities. For example, a leader meeting with the board of directors is likely of high importance, and the leader will give his or her time, energy, and attention to the meeting. On the other hand, if the leader is meeting with a group of employees that he or she has met with before and believes they won't ask any good questions or provide important input, the leader will likely deem this meeting low importance, and he or she will devote less attention, time, and energy to it. In the Avcor example, Nancy placed a high level of importance on communicating, whereas the new leader didn't.

> The perception of the importance of the communication event determines how much time and energy a leader is willing to give it.

Lack of trust

Trust is derived from the German word *trost,* meaning comfort or being comfortable with. It's the thermometer of individual or group health and the gauge that determines willingness on the part of the employee to communicate with leadership.

Stephen MR Covey, in his book, *The Speed of Trust: The One Thing That Changes Everything,* expresses the importance of trust in a powerful way:

There is one thing, which if removed, will destroy the most successful business, the most influential leadership, the greatest friendship, the strongest character, and the deepest love. That one thing is trust. It undergirds and affects the quality of every relationship, every communication, every work project, every collaboration, and every effort in which we are engaged.

If employees don't trust leaders' intentions or don't feel safe in expressing their questions, thoughts, or concerns, they'll limit what they communicate and how they communicate. Employees begin to feel communicating any form of dissension or disagreement with leaders is taking a big risk, so they remain silent. Employees discuss issues behind closed doors rather than with leadership. They talk about leadership, but don't talk to leadership.

What contributes to no trust? The possibilities are numerous. According to a survey of leaders at 215 companies conducted by Manchester, Inc. in 2001, the following behaviors lead to no trust:

- Acting inconsistently or communicating mixed messages
- Communicating with negative intent
- Withholding information
- Telling a half-truth or lie
- Being self-serving
- Being closed-minded or having to be right
- Being disrespectful to others
- Failing to support others.
- Betraying confidences
- Breaking promises
- Being insincere
- Transferring blame to others rather than taking responsibility
- Acting in a manner inconsistent with stated values
- Hurt someone with words or actions and fails to reconcile
- Playing favorites or applying inconsistent standards

If you look at the Avcor example, many of these led to the employees becoming quiet.

> **What occurs if employees don't trust leadership?**

The fallacy of the open door

In group sessions with leaders, we often ask, "How many of you have an open-door policy?" Most, if not all, hands go up, and we can see that the participants seem proud that they have one. Our response is straight-forward: "Having an open door policy means *nothing.*"

Leaders may be effective communicators, but if coworkers or employees shy away from approaching the open door or sharing their thoughts and feelings with the leader, something is missing. The true measure of inclusion is this: Are employees willing to come through the door? Are they willing to communicate with the leader?

> Don't pride yourself on having an open-door policy. Pride yourself on the number of people who come through your door.

What determines whether employees are willing to come through the open door? The reason is primarily what's happened in past interactions between leaders and employees.

So the question becomes: "What do leaders do consciously or unconsciously that decreases the level of trust, closes the open door, and diminishes the opportunity to experience a culture of inclusion?"

What was discovered from interviews with employees in many ways mirrored the work of Jack R. Gibb in his book, *Trust: A New View of Personal*

Organizational Development. He was the originator of trust-level theory and the primary proponent of the importance of trust in organizational behavior. Gibb identified certain leadership behaviors that decreased the level of trust. His findings, as well as our research, identify the following actions that stop employees from coming through the open door.

Employees stop coming through the open door when a leader:

- is perceived as *judging;*
- creates a persona of *superiority;*
- is seen as *certain;*
- is perceived as *overcontrolling;* or
- appears *indifferent.*

Here, we review each of these in more detail.

Judging

When employees perceive a leader as judging employees, trust is diminished and employees are less likely to communicate openly and honestly. *Judging* occurs when a leader jumps to the conclusion that what the employee is saying or doing is wrong. The leader quickly makes a statement that stops the employee's question, point of view, or ideas from being expressed. For example:

- "You can't get your priorities straight."
- "That was a dumb question."
- "You're not experienced enough."
- "Come back when you have the right answer."

The leader may be abrupt and prescribe how the employee should think or what the employee should do. After that point, the leader fails to hear anything being said, which can make the employee feel discounted. In other words, the employee's point of view doesn't count.

When a leader takes this form of communication, employees often say things like, "He didn't give me a chance to explain," "She tends to shoot the messenger," or "I hate to bring up something that isn't going well, because blame will be directed my way."

Judging also reflects on what's referred to as the *fundamental attribution error.* First described by Lee Ross, a Stanford University professor of humanities and sciences, it represents a person's tendency to place undue emphasis on internal characteristics to explain someone else's behavior in a given situation.

For example, a leader observes and then attributes a judgment to that observation. Sue is late for a meeting. This is an observable fact, but then the leader attributes to this observation a judgment: "She's not very responsible." This isn't necessarily fact. The story in the leader's assessment leads to negative feelings about the employee, which in turn guides the way the leader will act in response to the original action. The leader attributes actions to the employee's disposition rather than looking at the situation that may have caused the employee to be late. Instead of concluding something is wrong with Sue, the leader should ask, "Why would Sue, who usually is prompt, be late?" Doing so avoids the attribution error.

If employees see a leader as judgmental, they'll learn not to step through the open door.

Superiority

When a leader exhibits a persona of *superiority,* the leader is essentially saying, "I'm better, smarter, wiser, or more important than you." The leader uses his or her position of authority, educational degree, or experience as a means to establish that he or she is right and that the employee can't be right because of his or her inadequacies. This approach has a sense of one-upmanship. Examples include the following:

- "I don't agree and I've been around here a lot longer than you."
- "I hold a degree in that area so I should know."
- "If you'd listened to what I tried to tell you in the beginning, we wouldn't be sitting around here now trying to make sense out of this."

Why would an employee want to come through the open door when a leader is exhibiting superiority?

Another form of superiority occurs when the leader choses to criticize an employee in front of others. The employee is in an uncomfortable position and often hurt by what the leader says. Other employees who have witnessed this situation soon learn to be cautious and safe when around the leader.

Certainty

When a leader is seen as certain, the leader is perceived saying, "My mind's made up. Don't confuse me with the facts." The leader gives the impression that he or she knows all the answers and doesn't need or desire any additional information, which relates closely to what is referred to as having a fixed mindset. A leader who is intolerant of other people's views, closed minded, and inflexible has a *fixed mindset.* The leader has a high need to be right, even to the point of winning an argument rather than solving a problem. Here are some examples:

- "I know what I'm talking about, so no need to get into the rationale."
- "I have all the information I need, and I've made my decision."
- "I know what's best for you, and it's not working on that project."
- "I don't want to hear about it; I know what I want to do."

Ask yourself the question, "Do I ever get frustrated when a person isn't open to my ideas or thinking, especially when I know the information I hold could be of great value to the other person?"

Again, when a leader is described as fixed in his or her thinking, employees stop making the attempt to share their concerns, point of view, or ideas.

Controlling

When the leader is seen as *controlling,* the impression is the leader is trying to change or restrict employees' behavior or attitude by imposing his or her own way of doing things on them. The leader feels the need to impose controls in order to manage the deficiencies of those he or she manages.

How do you respond to the statements? Check the ones that describe how you think about managing:

_____ I often feel I should know more than the people who report to me.

_____ I think of myself as the problem solver.

_____ I find it difficult, if not impossible, to say no to a worthy cause or person requesting my involvement.

_____ I heroically drag myself to an important meeting even when stressed out rather than delegating the job to a junior member of my team.

_____ I receive a constant string of phone calls, texts, and emails, even during the evenings or on the weekend.

_____ I find it's often easier to do the work myself than teach someone else to do it.

_____ I feel I'm responsible for my constituency, for the goals in my area of responsibility, and for our success.

_____ I find myself in the middle of others' conflicts.

If you checked several of them, you're more than likely seen as controlling.

David Bradford and Allan Cohen, in their book, *Managing for Excellence: The Guide to Developing High Performance in Contemporary Organizations* describe what they refer to as the "heroic manager." The heroic manager holds a set of beliefs that lead to controlling behavior. Some examples of what the heroic manager believes are as follows:

- The heroic manager believes "I am supposed to know." He or she may say: "As the manager, I should know more than the employees who work for me. I'm in the position I am in because of what I know."

This attitude plays out in a variety of ways. If the manager believes he or she should know more than the employees who work for him or her, the manager will tell more than ask. To ask may imply the manager doesn't know. The heroic manager may refrain from sharing information, believing the more he or she shares, the more likely employees may discover what the manager doesn't know. Perhaps the worst grievance occurs when the manager hires individuals that he or she knows don't know as much as the manager does. A heroic manager will often want all the details and know everything that is going on so he or she can feel in the know. Consequently, the manager becomes a micromanager.

- The heroic manager believes "I'm supposed to solve problems." He or she may say, "I'm measured on the quality of my solutions. Bring your problems to me, and I'll get them solved. If I involve others, they simply slow down the process and get in the way." When employees begin to realize the manager is there to solve the problems, they readily bring their problems or needs to the manager to be solved rather than taking personal responsibility for solving their own problems or needs.

- The heroic manager believes "I'm responsible." He or she may say, "If we have a good month, I'm responsible. If we have a bad month, I'm responsible. If the meeting goes well, I'm responsible; if not, I'm responsible."

When this is occurring, the manager becomes over-responsible. Employees then feel under-responsible leading to disengagement.

The greatest fear of a heroic manager is losing control. Consequently, he or she compensates by overcontrolling. Examples of what you may hear and what the manager may be thinking include the following:

- "Let me tell you how to do your job." (Then I won't have to worry about it.)
- "I need to see all the detail." (Then I'll feel safe if asked.)
- "I'll take care of it for you." (Then I'll know.)

If a leader is controlling, employees feel like they're being contained in a small box and not told what to do. They become quiet.

Indifference

Have you ever been in a situation where a leader has made you feel unimportant? Have you ever been in a situation where it appeared the leader wasn't listening? Have you ever felt that what is important to you isn't to the leader? Have you ever had a leader change the subject in the middle of what you thought was an important conversation? In each case, the employee experiences indifference and often interprets the leader's action as not caring. *Indifference* occurs when employees sense a lack of interest in them. They don't feel validated (we discuss this more in chapter seven).

Today's technology has increased this perception of indifference when a leader's cell phone buzzes in the middle of a conversation and he or she takes the call or checks the message while the employee is trying to have a conversation—often referred to as multitasking.

Examples of behavior indicating indifference are as follows:

174

- Not listening
- Being preoccupied
- Not demonstrating any form of interest
- Disrupting or postponing crucial conversations

If employees don't feel the leader cares about them, they become quiet. In many cases, the lack of interest is why employees chose to quit and leave.

Creating a Culture of Inclusion

Up to this point we have focused on what quiets the organization. The emphasis has been on what leadership does without malice or intent that contributes to disengagement. Our attention now transitions to what leadership can do to create a culture of inclusion, where voices are heard, employees are involved, and leaders can take pride in the number of employees coming through their door. In order to reengage or maintain high engagement, the element of inclusion is vital.

How information is gathered, shared, disseminated, and understood greatly impacts the sense of inclusion as does whether individuals feel they have the freedom to openly express themselves. A lack of information flow is one of the fastest ways to create disengaged employees. If employees don't feel included, they won't feel engaged.

The following is an example of a company, Wenck Associates, an environmental engineering firm, which exhibits high employee engagement and high work satisfaction. Wenck Associates has been awarded as one of the best places to work for its size category for eight consecutive years.

As you read through this case, underline the various ways that the company has created a culture of inclusion.

Wenck Associates

If you ask the Joe Grabowski, the former president of Wenck Associates, what his key responsibilities were, he'll tell you that one of them was to inform and be informed by associates. When asked why he refers to employees as "associates" or "members," his response is, "I wanted them to feel like equal members of an open community." For him, informing others is demonstrated in many ways, and is still carried on after Joe's departure. First of all, everyone gets a copy of the strategic plan. Embedded in this plan are the company's vision, mission, and purpose. Town hall meetings allowed employees to get clarity on or question the strategic plan and its implications. Employees can use the compelling company website to stay current on organizational happenings, access a variety of information sources, and by just typing in a word, connect to a collection of resources available for experience and support. How the organization is doing on a monthly basis is posted, and at least once a month the president or a senior officer has an open information session with anyone who cares to attend. Once a year, they have an all-hands meeting that everyone from every geographic location attends. This event provides a variety of opportunities to share, learn, better under-stand, and connect with colleagues.

The expectation to learn is ever-present. Walking around the company, you see posters announcing various bag lunch seminars where employees share new engineering practices or a recent customer experience.

Being informed occurs in a variety of venues. Every Friday morning, employees meet with senior management to ask questions and share insights (donuts provided). Formal surveys are conducted on how the company is doing regarding a series of factors, such as customer service, leadership, learning, and communication; any item that scores below ninety percent in terms of satisfaction is immediately addressed. Limited-duration teams are formed to work on and provide recommendations regarding a given strategic goal. Team members present their recommendations to the executive board and are asked to remain involved as the issues are discussed. Employees are assigned a facilitator (someone who isn't their direct manager). The facilitator is there to mentor, coach, and provide guidance and listen deeply to the concerns and challenges of the employee.

When asked what practices contribute to winning the award for one of the best places to work, a key response is always, "We have a culture of inclusion."

> **Could any of these inclusion strategies work in your organization?**

Using Wenck Associates as an example, the following are various forms of inclusion:

Information sharing

Inclusion occurs when information is shared. At Wenck Associates, all employees received the five-year strategic plan in a booklet format. Grabowski visits every location and overviews the plan, seeks input, and answers questions. Associates feel well informed regarding the organization's direction, focus, and goals.

Grabowski would be the first to admit information sharing is a challenge to manage. Too much sharing can overwhelm some employees, whereas others feel enough information can never be shared. One also has to be mindful of how the information will be interpreted.

Information sharing has also gone digital and can take the form of emailing, blogging, websites, wikis, podcasting, forums, images, newsgroups, and so on.

Inviting input

Inclusion occurs when employees feel they have the opportunity to weigh in on key matters that impact them and/or the business, usually in the form of surveys and focus groups. Inviting employees to share their thoughts and opinions is equally important. In its simplest form, inviting is asking rather than telling. Yet, inviting requires the leader to be genuine and truly open to others. If not, the organization quickly quiets.

Inviting is also important because every organization has an element of the population that is low assertive and quiet by nature. Those employees feel comfortable saying little. Yet, they have valuable information to share. What they want is to be asked. When asked, these employees readily share their thoughts and feelings.

Providing feedback

Inclusion occurs when employees know how the organization is doing. They welcome any form of posted or shared information that gives them clear indicators of how they're doing. For example, if you walk through the BMW sports utility vehicles manufacturing plant in High Point, South Carolina, you would see various monitors continuously update employees with real-time information on production, quality, and safety.

Using teams

Inclusion occurs when employees feel they're a part of a team that contributes to solving a problem or advancing a strategy. Engagement increases when employees feel they contribute. For example, Skanska USA Building, a Swedish construction management company, uses what it refers to as "limited duration teams." These teams are given a problem to solve, a challenge to address, or a strategy to execute. They're given a short window of time to complete and make a recommendation to the senior leadership team. This practice provides a larger segment of the employee population the opportunity to get involved and help author the organization's future.

Allowing for mutual influence

Mutual influence occurs when the leader has the ability and willingness to influence his or her team or associates and they in turn have an opportunity to influence the leader. This culture of openness allows information to be readily shared. However, mutual influence can get out of balance. If a leader overly influences his or her team or associates, a compliance culture can happen. Employees find themselves having to say yes when they want to say no. If this occurrence is frequent, apathy grows, and few conversations happen that question the leader's decision. Team members or associates give up trying to influence their leader.

On the other hand, if the team holds the power to overly influence the leader, the leader loses his or her voice in matters and is often labeled weak. Overly playing the need for consensus contributes to this possibility.

When both parties can influence each other and there is an attitude of listening first to input before deciding, inclusion increases.

Building trust

The previous examples are a few ways to increase inclusion. However, the most important element to a culture of inclusion is trust in each other. In order for these inclusion practices to have any real value, leaders need to be trusted. Employees need to feel safe in order to feel comfortable expressing themselves. What can leadership do to create trust? The following are some of the practices that can lead to increased trust:

Disclosing

In order to build trust, you should disclose. To do so, demonstrate openness, share feelings as well as thoughts, be vulnerable, be honest with information, admit mistakes, and let employees know the personal side of who is leading them.

Making it safe

Another person will only share his or her real thoughts, concerns, or beliefs if he or she feels safe. If both the leader and the employee feel safe, they can talk about almost anything. Indicators alert when a person is unsafe. Look for conditions like avoidance, uneasiness, defensive posture, and reluctance to share. If you observe any of these conditions, describe to the other person what is occurring, ask if you are doing something that is making the person uncomfortable, and invite him or her to share his or her thoughts and feelings.

Honoring the absent

Stephen MR Covey, in his book, *The Speed of Trust: The One Thing That Changes Everything,* identifies honoring the absent as a way to build trust. How do you talk about others in their absence? If in the absence of colleagues, you speak negatively of them and in various ways discount or judge them, they may begin to ponder what you say about them when they aren't present.

Practicing realistic optimism

We talked in chapter three that one of the most important roles of a leader is to define reality—what is happening in the business and the challenges and opportunities that are occurring. Defining reality speaks to disclosing and being candid and straightforward with people.

It also demonstrates a positive, optimistic view that encourages others to engage.

Demonstrating your integrity

A definition of integrity is keeping the promises or commitments you make to others, even the small ones that aren't necessarily visible to others. Integrity is about character. Does your walk mirror your talk?

Resting your personality

Often leaders are seen leading with their personality. For example, if by nature the leader is assertive, he or she will tend to want to tell. The best way to rest one's personality is to ask and listen.

Practicing reciprocity

If a leader listens, the employee is likely to listen. If the leader shares feelings, the employee is more likely to share his or her feelings. If the leader is open and interested, the employee is more likely to be open and interested. If the leader extends trust, the employee is more likely to extend trust to the leader.

Demonstrating openness

Mutual influence occurs when there is a balance between the leader's ability to influence employees and the employees' ability to influence the leader. Make conscious efforts to provide venues that demonstrate an open versus fixed mindset.

As trust increases, the opportunity to include others in a productive manner increases. In many ways, the organization becomes noisy rather than quiet.

Stepping through the Open Door

Earlier in this chapter, we discussed how certain behaviors can close the open door. Opposite behaviors encourage employees to come through the open door. They also represent ways to increase a culture of inclusion.

The opposite of *judging* is when the leader is seen as *describing*.

Instead of making judgments, the employee sees the leader as requesting information about the employee's ideas. The leader seeks to better understand the employee's point of view rather than to judge it. The employee sees the leader as listening to learn. Instead of discounting the messenger, the leader works to understand the message. Rather than making a statement of judgment, the leader makes attempts to clarify and understand. Examples include the following:

- "Let me try to understand why this problem occurred."
- "Describe for me what happened."
- "Let me get your perspective and then I'll share mine."

The opposite of *superiority* occurs when the leader makes employees feel like *equals*.

When the leader treats employees as an equal, there's a sense of mutual respect. They may have differences in talent, ability, power, and status, but if the leader exhibits an attitude of equality, these differences are of little importance. A comfortable context for dialogue is created. Some examples of this form of inclusion are as follows:

- "We're in this together."
- "I'm glad we have different viewpoints. Since we're on the same team, we have a better chance of covering all angles."
- "While I have spent a lot of time in that discipline, I'd like to hear your ideas."

The opposite of *certainty* occurs when the leader is described as *open*. The leader possesses an adaptive mindset described as flexible, tolerant of others' views, and easy to talk with.

When the leader is open, he or she is willing to learn, to see others' points of view, and to adapt. Here are some examples:

- "What do you see as the key issue here?"
- "Let's hear your ideas."
- "You're right. That's a better idea."

The person with an open attitude is seen as investigating issues rather than taking sides on them.

The opposite of *overcontrolling* is when employees see the leader as *empowering* them. The key becomes freeing up others and giving them responsibility rather than taking it from them.

When the leader asks questions and seeks information, the leader has no predetermined solution, attitude, or method to impose. The leader demonstrates a desire to work with employees and to empower them. Some examples include the following:

- "We have a problem, and I need your help."
- "You know the topic better than I do, so take the lead."
- "I trust you. Let me know if you need help."

The opposite of *indifference* is when the leader demonstrates *interest*. This is the most important of the five behaviors—showing interest in the employee's ideas and concerns. When the leader demonstrates interest, the employee feels validated and important because the leader is giving him or her his undivided attention. The leader doesn't allow anything to interfere with the conversation. The leader demonstrates interest in what the employee has to say. The leader wants to understand the employee's position, feelings, or problems. Here are some examples:

- "I'm all ears. Share with me your thoughts on the project."
- "I'd like to know and understand your perspective on this matter."
- "Let's meet somewhere away from the many distractions I may have."

In summary, creating a culture of inclusion is more about willingness than ability. The willingness to communicate occurs because the leader has made it safe for the employee to come through his or her open door. The more employees sense true interest in them, the more they'll trust the communication encounter and the likelihood of their coming through the door increases. Leaders need to create the belief on the part

185

of others that they can be trusted with information, that they give energy to the communication process, and that they're good listeners who ask relevant questions, strive for understanding, and respond to the needs of others.

This table summarizes the preceding information:

A sense of inclusion is decreased when the leader. . .	A sense of inclusion is increased when the leader. . .
• Is perceived as judging	• Is seen as describing
• Creates a persona of superiority	• Creates equality
• Is seen as certain	• Is seen as open
• Is perceived as overcontrolling	• Is seen as empowering
• Appears indifferent	• Demonstrates interest

Chapter Summary

Inclusion naturally creates engagement. Suppressed communication naturally creates disengagement.

The manner in which information is gathered, disseminated, and understood greatly impacts a sense of inclusion, as does whether or not individuals feel they have the freedom to openly express themselves. A lack of information flow is one of the fastest ways to create disengaged employees. If employees don't feel included, they won't feel engaged.

To create a culture of inclusion, to look at how leadership can build into the culture a series of ways to share, include, involve, and hear from the constituency. Like the Wenck Environmental Engineering firm, develop ways to create inclusion. Make inclusion a top priority of leadership. Budget time and energy to this endeavor. Communication can't be seen as nice to do only when time permits. If you inject genuine optimistic energy into communicating, the energy in the organization increases.

The other key to inclusion is willingness. The most important factor in sharing information is having a culture of trust, which begins with trusting leadership. A true measure of inclusion is the evidence that information sharing is occurring at all levels. Look at your own behaviors and ask yourself the question, "Am I opening or shutting my open door?" How do you make sure your employees are willing to come through the open door?

In our next chapter, we'll explore the next of the five elements of engagement: The Element of Validation.

Chapter 7

The Element of Validation

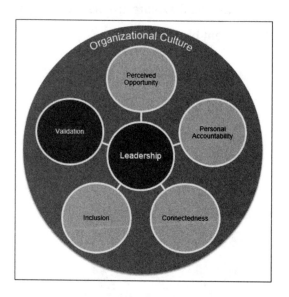

Premise: Engagement occurs when employees feel that they matter and that they have a valued place in the organization.

Avcor's new president was focused on transforming the business from generic products to a custom software consulting business. All his energy was focused on executing a plan that would have the organization positioned to begin this new business model within six months. While he prepared for the new beginning, many employees still dealt with what had ended. Many employees still lived in the loss, not sure how they fit into the new business focus.

Because the leaders put all their energy into building the consulting business, the employees felt their needs and concerns were being overlooked, even neglected. They also felt that they weren't personally supported. Leadership didn't appear interested in them.

Before the acquisition, employees felt leadership cared about and supported them. In various ways, they knew where to go for help. Under Nancy's leadership, strong emphasis was placed on personal development; employees felt they had opportunities to learn and grow. The strong focus on executing the strategic change now currently over-shadowed most of the developmental initiatives. Employees questioned whether they mattered. It was hard to stay engaged.

Defining Validation

Validation is the expressed interest leaders have in their employees. From the employees' perspective, being validated is when they feel like the leader sees them as important. There is something about the way the leader engages with them that makes them feel like they matter, as a person, not just as employees. They feel validated because the leader demonstrates they truly matter to the leader.

Often you'll hear the question asked, "What are you doing to retain your high performers?" The more important question to ask is, "What are you doing to ensure you're retaining all your valued employees?"

The fact that people desire to know they have a valued place in the organization hit home recently in a conversation Tom had with Jeff, a young man in his late twenties preparing to leave his job. Tom was somewhat surprised because Jeff had spoken often about how much he enjoyed the work he was doing. He worked in retail, and many of the employees were of similar age and fun to associate with. The culture had a positive vibe, and the employees believed in the products. For these reasons, Jeff took great delight in working with customers.

Jeff was so engaged and energized that he sought out opportunities to increase his knowledge about the business. He took on additional tasks and served as a peer leader to other employees on the floor. The newer people often came to Jeff for help and support in how to handle certain customer issues.

Believing he was already doing many of the things that managers did, Jeff decided to apply for a manager position when one opened. Even though he'd never had direct reports before, he was given the promotion. About a year in the role, Jeff concluded management wasn't his calling. He didn't feel comfortable with the day-to-day responsibility of managing people, so he asked to return to his old position.

This company valued employees who wanted to take on more responsibility and move up in the organization. Having someone ask to move down, not up, was unusual, but nonetheless, the company agreed. Jeff returned to his old position and continued with the same energy that he had previously. However, things were never the same for him. His manager, who previously had been supportive, became distant and paid little attention to him. Employees who previously came to him for help and support were told not to go to Jeff for answers but to go to their

190

managers instead. In essence, Jeff's development stopped, his perception of the value he contributed dropped, and consequently he began to question why he stayed.

When Tom asked Jeff why he ultimately decided to leave, his answer was directly tied to this premise: Jeff said he felt he had become invisible and that the managers couldn't care less about him. He stated he knew he still had a job, but that he no longer had *a valued place in the organization*. He knew it was time to move on.

> *Do your employees feel that they matter—that they have a valued place in the organization?*

According to Gallup's research, one of the most important actions that leadership can take to help ensure the organization's future success is to demonstrate interest in the development of the employees. Interest comes in a variety of forms: recognition, listening, involvement, understanding, rewards, learning, growth, and so on.

This chapter focuses on the importance of validation and introduces how leaders can demonstrate "acts of interest."

Why Employees Choose to Stay

Pfizer Global Research's leadership asked Steve to explore the increasing level of interest Pfizer had in understanding why talent chose to leave, how to retain key scientists, and how to develop bench strength. Rather than focus on traditional sources of information such as exit interviews, the decision was made to focus on why employees chose to stay rather than chose to leave. A quote by Tom Peters encouraged Steve: "Has anyone asked your employees what keeps them at your company? Why do we ask great questions in exit interviews, but neglect asking them early enough to make a difference in their decision to stay or leave the organization?"

Beverly Kaye and Sharon Jordan-Evans also influenced Steve. In their book, *Love 'Em or Lose 'Em, Getting Good Employees to Stay,* they explored the question: What factors determine employee retention? Their basic conclusion was simple: "Treat great employees like any other friends you want to keep: respect them, challenge them, value them, have fun with them, and do not tell them lies." Similarly, Steve was able to report to Pfizer senior leadership the key reasons that employees stayed and the opportunity this presented Pfizer leadership to respond proactively. Based on conducting extensive interviews with Pfizer employees, Steve identified the following reasons that led employees to choose to stay:

Quality of work life

One basic reason employees often stayed was referred to as "quality of work life," which involved compensation, physical environment, benefits, and amenities such as flex time, exercise facilities, and so on.

Frederick Herzberg, a pioneer of "job enrichment," is viewed as one of the great original thinkers in management and motivational theory. Herzberg pointed out that the absence of certain elements he referred to as "hygiene factors" (compensation, benefits, physical environment, matching contributions) leads to dissatisfied employees and the subsequent departure of talented employees. However, those factors are only half of the story. He noted that factors he called "motivators" (challenging work, recognition, opportunity to do something meaningful, growth opportunities, and a sense of importance in an organization) provided positive satisfaction.

What can you learn from this old lesson? It's important to provide key hygiene factors because they help to avoid dissatisfaction, but that alone won't cause employees to stay. Other factors that are closely aligned with the element of validation are necessary to truly help employees choose to stay, although important quality of work life wasn't the main reason employees stayed.

Pride, profit, and possibilities

Another key finding in the Pfizer study was described as the pride, profit, and possibilities scenario. *Pride* was the feeling employees had regarding who they worked for and the purposeful work that was conducted. The kind of research that was being done at Pfizer to serve humanity and the professional reputation the company held made up this factor.

Profit was an expression of the health of the organization in terms of sustainability and growth. Recall in chapter three we introduced the Three Stories. Retaining talent is much harder if the organization is experiencing Story One where the primary emphasis is on just surviving rather than in Story Three where the emphasis is on opportunity.

The third factor, *possibilities,* was a response to the organization's health. If the organization were healthy, employees believed all kinds of possibilities for growth would be present. Equally important, having the sense of possibility allowed employees to see their opportunity to engage in meaningful work. Although important, pride, profit, and possibilities weren't the main reason employees stayed.

Right work

A third area of importance was referred to as "right work." This occurred when the job itself brought a high level of personal satisfaction. Right of work represents the positive feelings an employee has about his or her work, including factors such as experiencing rewarding work, having a true sense of purpose, playing to one's strengths, and having the opportunity for expressing one's self through work, which we refer to as "playing one's music." Again, although important, this area also wasn't the main reason employees stayed.

Stability

A fourth important factor in staying was experiencing a sense of stability. The opposite of stability occurred when employees experienced a high level of flux or continuous change. Over time, as we discussed in chapter one, if the organization continues to experience churn, employees tend to put their energy on hold, making the choice to quit and stay or quit and leave. What can neutralize the positive perceptions the first three factors (quality of work life; pride, profit, possibilities; and right work) have on the decision to stay is *flux*. It's notable how often a well-known organization disappears off the annual employer-of-choice listing after a company began to experience a high degree of flux. Employees didn't like working in a state of constant change and uncertainty, but again, although important, this factor wasn't the most influential.

Demonstrated interest

The factor that had the greatest impact was both simple and profound: Employees want to know that their manager shows a demonstrated interest in them and validates them. Validation is arguably the most important element of engagement because it personally influences each individual in the organization. Showing interest is critical to retaining and reengaging employees.

At one point in Steve's career, he was asked to form a start-up company focused on developing interactive video to be used as part of a leadership development curriculum. He needed help so he sought out some talented individuals who had demonstrated a real understanding of this emerging technology and who were experts in leadership development or curriculum design. To his delight, everyone he contacted accepted his invitation to join this emerging start-up even though doing so involved stepping out of good jobs.

What was interesting was why they left. Most of the talent came from an organization that at that time had experienced a significant amount of flux including turnover at the top. One of the talented new employees when asked by Steve why he left stated: "I was in the elevator going up to the floor I worked when the president of the organization stepped in beside me. His office was on the same floor. The whole time in the elevator, he didn't say a word to me. I don't think he even knew my name." He didn't feel the president cared about him, wasn't interested in finding out who he was, or didn't care about what he did. He didn't feel validated. This one encounter was an influencing factor in his decision to leave.

> Always remember, employees will often forget what you say or do, but they will always remember how you made them feel.

As a leader, consider how you would answer the following:

- In your work culture, what are the ways employees are currently made to feel important and valued?
- How often do you take the opportunity to demonstrate interest in your employees?
- What do you do when a valued employee announces he or she is leaving?
- How do you reward employees?
- Do you know what makes your employees feel validated?

Acts of Interest

Validation is demonstrating, as leaders, that you care about your employees' well-being. The best way to demonstrate caring is through "acts of interest." Three primary acts can become part of the element of validation:

- Supporting the individual as a person and for the work he or she does.
- Rewarding the individual with both monetary and natural rewards.
- Developing the individual by providing opportunities to learn and grow.

The following model illustrates supporting, rewarding, and developing employees:

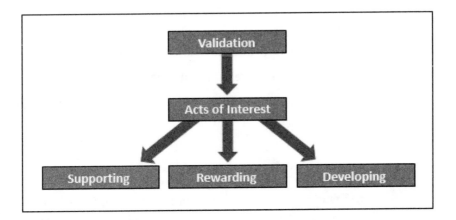

Supporting the individual as a person and for the work he or she does

One of the questions employees often have on their mind is, "Where do I go for help?" A leader can support the individual in many ways, such as the following:

- Providing additional help with a complex project that is overwhelming the employee.
- Helping make connections with key people as a way to make the employee more visible.
- Helping in a personal family situation when daycare cancels due to weather.
- Being a good listener.
- Being an advocate in the employee's absence.
- Supporting a balanced work life.

In each case, the employee feels validated because of the support others personally provide and for the work he or she does.

Types of support

One way for leaders to increase their effectiveness in the area of support is to understand there are different types of support. This table includes four types of support and thoughts about what leaders can do to implement the different types:

Type of support	What leaders can do
Motivation The willingness to perform	Help people feel motivated, show confidence, delegate meaningful tasks, and ensure contributions are recognized.
Capability The individual's ability to perform well, including the knowledge and skills required for high performance	Provide exposure to information and knowledge or find a mentor to help people build a particular skill.
Resources The tools, materials, and information that support performance	You may find the resources that employees need within your own function or area. In many situations, you may need to identify and seek resources in other areas of the organization.
Processes The systems and processes that foster and support performance.	Check in with your work area and other functions to be certain that processes and procedures support performance. If the process is broken, find a solution and fix it

Examples of support

Wenck Associates demonstrates support by providing employees with a mentor they refer to as a *facilitator.* All employees at every level in the organization have access to a facilitator, who in most cases isn't their direct supervisor or manager, but is more likely to be an associate, who, five years ago, was in a similar situation to the new employee. The facilitator can then share experiences or lessons learned, connect the employee to other experienced engineers, and help the employee avoid some of the pitfalls the facilitator encountered. Wenck believes having the facilitator accelerates the onboarding, development, and growth of new associates and also demonstrates personal interest in the employee.

At Skanska USA Building, an employee can ask for, or, at times, are assigned a coach with a focus on growing his or her leadership potential. The coaches observe the leader in action and have knowledge of best practices in organizational and leadership behavior. The role of the coach is to support the employee's career advancement. Skanska believes this form of support builds bench strength that contributes to the long-term sustainability of the business.

Personal interest

Whether it's providing resources or removing obstacles, everyone needs support to perform effectively. Larry Wilson, the founder of Wilson Learning Corporation, had a wonderful phrase: "I have to do it myself, and I can't do it alone."

The type of support you provide is clearly secondary to the fact that you're demonstrating a personal interest in your employees. Sometimes all people need is to know that you understand what's going on in their lives and that you support them.

What are the various ways you can support your employees and peers?

Rewarding the individual with both monetary and natural rewards

How do you reward your employees? For most employees some form of monetary reward is still the primary means of recognition for performance, usually in the form of pay raises or bonuses. These rewards are referred to as *fixed*. However, a financial reward or promotion may not always provide the kind of recognition the situation calls for. For example, a company often gives monetary rewards in the form of a bonus paid at the end of the year. Although important, the employee may interpret this once-a-year form of recognition simply as additional compensation for meeting goals. The sense of recognizing an employee for a specific goal met or having in some manner contributed to the success of the organization at a specific time may be lost. At times, this form of reward can become an expectation and actually serve as a demotivator if not received, one of the things Herzberg pointed out in his discussion of hygiene factors stated earlier. Employees feel that the organization is taking the compensation away from them.

Another form of reward is promoting an individual who has demonstrated in some form a readiness to go to the next level within the organization. The recognition comes in the form of a new title or role. Although a powerful form of recognition, in some cases, no promotion opportunities are available. What then becomes available to the organization to reward the individual? One strategy is to create a new box on the organization chart or provide a new title. A second strategy is simply to increase the employee's level of compensation.

Is your organization stuck in a pay-for-performance mindset?

If the organization's mindset is on fixed rewards, the organization may overlook other ways to recognize employees. Our research indicates employees want to be recognized for the day-to-day activities that demonstrate their value to the organization. They aren't looking for money; they're simply looking for acknowledgment and to feel validated. When an employee demonstrates high performance or behaves in ways that support the values of the organization, he or she should be acknowledged. If nothing happens, the organization loses the opportunity to validate the employee. When employees go the extra mile on a project or have pitched in to help a colleague, what form of recognition applies?

Using Natural Rewards to Validate Employees

A second form of reward always available to the leader and in most cases doesn't involve money is referred to as natural rewards. *Natural rewards* are forms of recognition an employee finds intrinsically satisfying about their work.

One example of a natural reward is *learning*. Learning is a reward that the organization can build into the employee's work life in the form of new experiences, seminars, books, mentoring, and so on. Another natural reward is *inclusion.* Including an employee in relevant meetings where he or she feels involved can be rewarding. A natural reward is a letter from a satisfied customer, a special thank you, and so forth.

What is important to realize is that not all natural rewards are the same for everyone. One employee may want to be rewarded with an opportunity to take on additional responsibilities that broaden his or her expertise, whereas another employee may want some form of public recognition for his or her accomplishments. Therefore, the key becomes discovering what is unique to each employee. One mistake leaders often make is to practice the golden rule. In this case, leaders take pride in believing they treat employees the way the leader wants to be treated, which assumes employees need what the leader needs. Treating others the way the way the leader wants to be treated is much more effective. Doing so requires a deeper understanding of who your employees are.

How are employees naturally rewarded in your organization?

Natural rewards become a form of payoff that make employees feel good about the work they do. When natural rewards aren't present, engagement diminishes. The work that employees do becomes a job with little sense of fulfillment. For example, if an employee considers recognition important but the leader provides little recognition, then employee dissatisfaction can increase. Even worse is paying attention to employees only when they have done something wrong and giving no recognition when something positive is accomplished.

The key to utilizing natural rewards is discovering what is unique to each individual. Beverly Kaye and Sharon Jordan-Evans in their book, *Love 'Em or Lose 'Em, Getting Good Employees to Stay,* introduced the importance of natural rewards. Their research focused on employees who had stayed with their organizations for more than five years. The question they posed to these employees was simple: "Why do you stay?" Their responses seldom suggested it was just for the money. Their responses reflected how they expressed the benefits in staying. Most often the benefit was a natural reward: informal environment, mentoring, relationships, respect, mission, and so on.

Steve worked to duplicate their work with his research with Pfizer Global Research and Development on why talent stays. He asked the same question to employees who had been with Pfizer for more than five years: "Why do you choose to stay?" Responses were consistent with Kaye and Jordan-Evans' findings. From these two sources of research, Steve created the following list of natural rewards that captures the main reasons people find satisfaction regarding their work and why they chose to stay:

- **Challenge:** Frequently presented with the opportunity to create or complete challenging projects that provide achievement or accomplishment.
- **Acknowledgment:** Recognition of goals met or exemplary performance in work. Receiving credit when credit is due. Recognized by others for expertise.

- **Team spirit:** Being a valued member of the team; a positive, friendly, collaborative work culture that supports positive behaviors.

- **Passion:** Having a reason to get up in the morning. Work allows the employee to deal with issues about which he or she has great interest, concern, and commitment.

- **Creativity:** Opportunity to do work that requires new ways of doing things; ability to take risks and get outside the box.

- **Informal environment:** Fun, enjoyable work environment where humor, laughter, and celebration regularly occur. Casual dress and relaxed atmosphere.

- **Freedom:** Independence and autonomy; ability to guide decisions regarding own projects; opportunity to select work activities that make sense.

- **Self-expression:** Encouraged and supported to fully express talents. Recognized for individual aptitudes and unique qualities.

- **Contribution:** Opportunity to have a direct impact on others and on the organization's success. Make a lasting legacy.

- **Meaning:** Opportunities to pursue a meaningful task. Strong sense of purpose or mission; work worthy of time and energy.

- **Security:** A job that isn't likely to be eliminated; some assurance of career destiny and rewards.

- **Leadership:** Confidence in leaders' abilities to anticipate and guide decisions or developing the employee's leadership capacity and taking opportunities to lead.

- **Workspace:** Healthy, positive work environment; workspace conducive to productivity; aesthetically pleasing space.

- **Mission:** Work that helps people or improves things; the feeling that work contributes to ideals.

- **Courage:** Support for bold ideas, a listening culture; open dialogue encouraged. Easy to put hard issues on the table.

- **Balance:** Work leaves time for pursuits outside of work. Work activities honor family, community, and other pursuits; lifestyle-friendly culture.

- **Adventure:** Work environment provides situations with excitement and flair; frequent risk taking with possible loss or gain encouraged.

- **Clear feedback:** The question, "How am I doing?" is clearly answered. Progress toward goals is noted and acknowledged. Positive feedback is given.

- **Mentoring:** Opportunity to mentor the development of others or to be mentored by wise people.

- **Entrepreneurship:** To engage in work that directly impacts success of a product or business. Receiving rewards through sense of invention or ownership.

- **Respect:** Respected by colleagues and managers; opinions and ideas sought by others.

- **Relationships:** Sense of belonging; opportunity to develop close friendships; frequent/open interpersonal contact.

- **Excellence:** Be the best; work allows for the pursuit of mastery and the development of new and existing capacities. Opportunities for development and learning encouraged.

> Within your work culture there may be other natural rewards that employees would express as reasons why they stay. Discover them.

Reward clusters

These natural rewards represent four clusters that make work fulfilling for employees. The clusters are meaning, lifestyle choice, connection, and mastery.

At various stages of an individual's work life, one of the four clusters may assume greater significance. Early on in one's career, mastery may be the most important. Later, connectedness emerges. Over time, lifestyle choice may become the highest priority, and even later meaning takes on greater prominence in what's important to the employee.

Meaning

Meaning is the opportunity an employee feels when his or her work is seen in the context of a worthwhile cause. Meaning is the feeling of being on a purposeful path that is worth one's time and energy—that one is on a valuable mission or calling. The rewards that fall into this category are meaning, contribution, mission, and passion.

Lifestyle choice

Lifestyle choice is the opportunity an employee feels to choose work activities, workspaces, and work styles that fit his or her life. The feeling of choice is the feeling of being free to bring one's whole self to work. The rewards that fall into this category are time, freedom, security, workspace, balance, and adventure.

Connection

A sense of *connection* is the relationship the employee has with others in the work environment. This feeling of alignment with people creates a sense of community at work. Shared values are being honored, and the employee is given voice in areas that affect him or her. The rewards that fall in to this category are team spirit, informal environment, leadership, courage, mentoring, respect, and relationships.

Mastery

A sense of *mastery* is the accomplishment an employee feels when competently performing tasks. The feeling of mastery involves the sense one is doing high quality work and that the opportunity exists to become an expert in a given area. The rewards that fall into this category are challenge, acknowledgment, creativity, self-expression, and excellence.

Natural rewards inventory

The Inventure Group where Steve was a co-founder along with Richard Leider, a highly regarded executive coach and author, undertook a third step. They created the natural rewards inventory, which a leader can use with employees to aid in identifying what natural rewards are most important to the employee's fulfillment. We include this inventory with instructions in chapter eight.

Why are natural rewards so important?

There is absolutely no argument that money-related rewards are important to people. As we stated earlier, in today's corporate environment, many leaders talk about how difficult it is to provide monetary rewards. They often say monetary rewards are less available than before and that they don't control the monetary rewards.

We want to point out these three important points about natural rewards:

- Leaders have a high degree of control over the usage of them. For the most part, leaders don't need a budget to be able to use natural rewards because the rewards have intrinsic, not monetary, value to the employee.
- Leaders can use natural rewards on an ongoing basis. They can have a tremendous impact on sustaining performance over time as well as the fulfillment and engagement of employees.
- Every individual defines what is rewarding. You can't decide for someone else what is rewarding to him or her. Say you rewarded someone with a new challenge, if he or she doesn't find a new challenge rewarding defeats the purpose; therefore, it's critical that you understand what is rewarding to different employees and then work to provide those rewards for individuals.

In summary, *Harvard Business Review* sends out "The Management Tip of the Day," and on October 26, 2017, the tip was as follows:

Recognition is one of the most powerful tools a manager has, but not everyone wants their good work to be called out in the same way. Acknowledging employees' work is meant to make them feel special—and it's hard to feel special if a corporate procedure treats everyone the same way. Tailor your approach to each employees' preferences, and if you aren't sure what those are, ask.

Developing the Individual by Providing Opportunities to Learn and Grow

Humans are programmed to grow. Most employees want to continue to grow in knowledge, competence, experience, and responsibility. Employees grow in different ways, but to achieve high engagement, they want to feel that leadership is interested in their growth. They want to feel that possibilities for upward movement in the organization exist to develop mastery within their area of expertise.

The Wenck Way

Another example of why Wenck Associates has won awards for the best places to work for eight consecutive years is clear in the ways in which they develop their people. Wenck has three developmental tracks employees can follow:

- Track One is a mastery track where employees chose to focus on their area of technical expertise—water, air quality, or municipal. The desire is to develop a domain competency where they can develop into a nationally recognized expert in their field.
- Track Two is to become a resource manager. A resource manager heads one of the environmental disciplines and has responsibility both to expand the discipline and to lead the employees who fall under that discipline. In this track they take a leadership position, but stay within their engineering disciplines.

- Track Three is business operations. The employees have chosen to move out of their engineering discipline and be groomed for a generalist role, sharing responsibility for how the organization runs. This could be finance, project management, marketing, human resources, information technology, or as general manager of one of Wenck's locations.

At any time, employees can change tracks. Interestingly, when a poll was taken to assess what developmental track they would select to take, the majority chose Track One. They wanted to grow within their area of expertise, which is important, because many organizations will take a high performer out of his or her technical discipline to be a manager. They may not consider or realize the employee may want an opportunity to play to his or her strengths, improve his or her expertise, and achieve mastery without feeling he or she has to become a manager. Too often, employees feel that to be rewarded and succeed in the eyes of the organization, they have to take a formal managerial or leadership role.

Each employee has a personal developmental budget he or she can use to enhance his or her expertise, learning, or experience.

A formal leadership developmental process is provided to approximately fifteen employees a year. They're nominated for this opportunity, sent a letter of invitation to participate by the president, and, if they accept, begin a yearlong leadership development process. Thus far, everyone at Wenck has accepted the invitation.

They begin with a series of assessments and questionnaires followed by a formal interview by a panel consisting of the president, a consultant in the area of temperament, and a consultant in the area of leadership.

The interview attempts to discover the employee's aspirations, understand his or her leadership point of view, and review various assessments.

The panel then recommends a growth plan to the employee in the form of a detailed letter. The employee then meets again with the panel, and together they go over the letter. The employee then begins a yearlong developmental plan with full support by the president and consultants. At the end of the year they conduct a formal review and outline a new developmental plan for the second year.

Employees have expressed surprise that they're given this opportunity, followed by a deep appreciation for how Wenck is demonstrating interest in their development. Many have come from other engineering firms and often imply they hadn't previously experienced any formal developmental process and felt their former employer was happy only if they met their utilization rates. Many indicated that Wenck's culture and developmental processes were the reason they came there to work, and clearly, why they stay.

Skanska USA Building

Another example of a company that demonstrates interest in its employees is Skanska USA Building, a large construction management company. Skanska USA Building has every one of its top leaders assess their personnel on an annual basis using the well-known "nine-box system." The boxes represent varying degrees of performance (low, medium, high), which measures actual achievements of the employee, and potential (low, medium, high), which measures the potential for future success in more senior, more critical positions. Using leadership criteria, all direct reports are assessed ranging from low performance, low potential to high performance, high potential, and then placed on the grid. Leaders review each employee regarding strengths and weaknesses, and then they discuss a developmental plan for each employee. In this way all employees feel they have a sponsor looking out for their interests.

Always Growing

Whether it's a process that involves a career path and/or job changes like Wenck or individual development plans like Skanska USA Building, leaders need to help ensure employees are always growing and developing. In difficult and challenging times, employees need to feel supported and rewarded for their performance, but they also need to keep growing and developing by the leaders providing challenges, learning opportunities, and work experiences.

What allows you to grow? The ancient sages would tell their students, "To learn, seek difficulties." They didn't say, "Make the best of difficulties," or, "Avoid difficulties." Facing the difficult situation head on—indeed inviting and relishing it—is what allows you to grow. Leaders need to help employees face the difficult situations at work and support them to learn and grow from those challenges.

Demonstrating Interest: Asking

One of the simplest ways to demonstrate interest is simply to ask. Following are a series of questions that you can use to demonstrate to employees your interest in them and validate that they matter:

- What do you find fulfilling about your work?
- What would you love to have more time to do?

212

- Why do you choose to stay?
- Beyond money and benefits, what rewards you?
- Do any parts of your life or work feel out of balance?
- Do you frequently receive praise for doing good work?
- Do you believe your opinions count?
- What would you like to grow into and/or learn as a next step in your growth?
- What do you do best?
- Do you have the opportunity to do what you do best every day?
- Are there areas of your work that you want to master?
- Is your development encouraged?
- Think of a few situations in your work life when you loved what you were doing. Describe what was happening. What came easy for you? Do these situations still occur in your present work?
- Do you have certain talents that you feel aren't being utilized?
- Do you have the support you need to do your work?
- Do you get satisfying returns on your time investments?
- Do you know what is expected of you at work?
- Does the mission/purpose of the organization make you feel your job is important?
- Do you feel a sense of purpose in your work?
- Do you understand the why of what you do?
- When you've had a good day at work and you go home feeling highly satisfied, what was it about that day that made you enjoy it? How often does this satisfaction occur (seldom, on occasion, frequently)?
- What gets you excited about going to work?

Take the time to learn who your employees are. When you're meeting one-on-one with an employee, use a selection of these questions to demonstrate interest in your employee.

> Arguably the most important competence in engaging employees is the simplest:
>
> Show interest.

Chapter Summary

Leaders need to show interest in their employees by how they personally support, reward, and develop them. Invariably, some employees will leave the organization. Make sure the reason they leave isn't because they feel they don't matter.

> *From an organizational perspective, how do you ensure systems and processes are in place to reward, support, and develop employees?*

The following are a series of validation rules for leaders. Your role as a leader is to apply these rules as a positive step in maintaining or increasing employee engagement:

- Show interest in your employees by just listening.
- Understand the unique needs of your employees and think natural rewards.
- Provide plenty of feedback. Employees want to know how they're doing.

- Be realistic about their future and the aspirations they may hold.
- Help them master their area of expertise and help them become known for their abilities.
- Expose them to growth opportunities.
- Demonstrate your support for them as unique individuals.
- Make sure they see you as a resource, someone they can go to for help.

In the next chapter, we'll provide a set of common practices that a leader or leadership can instill within the culture of an organization that lead to reengagement or maintains high engagement.

Chapter 8

Creating a Culture of Engagement

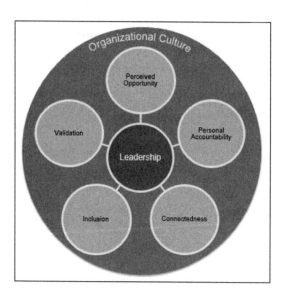

Premise: Sustainable engagement increases when the elements of engagement are infused in the culture rather than implemented as separate practices.

Arlene Blum, mountain climber and leader who led an American women's Himalayan expedition, provides a thoughtful introduction to this chapter: "The greatest rewards come from the greatest commitment."

How do you and/or the organization's leadership commit to creating a culture of high engagement? Or how do you and/or the organization's leadership commit to reengage an organization that has lost its energy? The simple answer is "Together."

The focus of this chapter will be to provide a set of common practices that a leader or leadership can instill within the culture of an organization that lead to reengagement or maintains high engagement. In some organizations, leaders just allow culture to happen. In others, leaders take an active, intentional role in shaping the kind of culture that encourages all employees to be engaged. This chapter will allow you that opportunity by providing worksheets for each of the five elements of engagement. The decision of what and how to influence the culture will come from you as a leader or as a part of leadership. Only you can make decisions about what you want your culture of engagement to be.

Focusing Leadership on Culture as the Context for Engagement

Several sources have looked at leadership development as a progression involving four levels:

- Creating a foundation of leadership
- Leading others
- Leading teams
- Shaping the work culture

Level one: Creating a foundation of leadership

Creating a foundation of leadership is the first level of development focused on the questions we covered in chapter two: "What do I want to be as a leader?" and, "What do I need to do as a leader?" The late Warren Bennis described becoming a leader as synonymous with becoming your "self." This level consists of two sub dimensions:

- Understand and clarify your core self (values, beliefs, purpose, legacy) in preparation for leading.
- Set the example through your actions.

> Level one is foundational to being a strong leader.

Unfortunately, many organizations don't sponsor or start their leadership development processes at this level. They fail to help individuals in positions of leadership develop their being. With no foundation, the leader simply uses his or her position of authority to get things done. Too often this leads to a culture of compliance rather than one of a committed followership. Too many organizations emphasize their leadership development beginning at level two.

Level two: Leading others

The focus at this level is on what a leader does for others, the constituency he or she serves. At this level, the leader learns various practices associated with leading: setting direction and goals, holding employees accountable, providing feedback, improving productivity, conducting meetings, and so on. The leader is focused on both the development and retention of employees as well as how they perform. This level is important because leadership is fundamentally a relationship between those who chose to lead and those who follow. Level two focuses on developing the necessary interactions that make others perform at a higher level.

Some leadership development goes no further than this level. Leaders become strong one-to-one managers. This has merit as long as the constituency the leader serves is relatively small and frequent opportunities for interaction with the leader are possible. This level becomes less effective as the number of direct reports increases. The leader discovers there just isn't enough time to adequately address the needs, objectives, and burdens of each employee. Employees become underserved and the leader becomes less effective.

Steve is currently coaching a vice president of a petroleum pipeline company who as a result of a major acquisition went from serving a group of ten direct reports to a group of two hundred. In order to survive and succeed, this leader needs to transition from thinking one-on-one to a more effective way of leading. The solution to this challenge of too many employees is to think more of leading one to group (level three) rather than just one-to-one.

Level three: Leading teams

Although one-on-one leadership is never left behind, a leader can become more effective if he or she emphasizes building a shared responsibility team among direct reports where natural teams work together and share responsibility for the function's outcomes, creating a collaborative culture and including larger numbers of employees in limited duration teams that work together on an opportunity or problem and provide their recommendations. This practice requires the leader to spend more time working with small groups or teams to accomplish specific outcomes. Having employees working together and being responsible for more than their job description allows the leader to play a more strategic role in how the business performs.

Level four: Shaping the work culture

This level often isn't a part of a leader's development. How do you as a leader take an active, intentional role in shaping the kind of culture that encourages those who call you their leader to be fully engaged? Rather than shape individuals, this level focuses on shaping the culture in a manner that instills certain practices and beliefs that lead to reengagement or sustain high engagement. These practices involve shaping what you want the organization to become using the five elements: creating a culture of opportunity, establishing a culture of personal accountability, identifying within the culture ways to include employees, creating a culture where key connections are made, and developing practices embedded in the culture focused on developing, recognizing, and supporting employees.

When implemented, the leader is able to sustain much of what is practiced in level two, managing others, even when the leader is absent. This sustainability happens because the practices are instilled in the culture and aren't driven solely by the leader's presence or actions.

This chapter focuses on level four and provides guidelines for shaping your culture.

220

Shaping Your Work Culture

What is culture? The Encarta Dictionary defines culture in the broad sense of "shared beliefs, customs, practices, and behaviors of a particular group of people." This very much fits our definition: "Culture occurs when the organization shares certain beliefs, norms, practices, and customs that are common to the majority of employees."

Culture exists in every organization in two aspects:

- **Formal:** Represented by the company's mission statements, values, or guidelines in an employee handbook, or defined policies and procedures
- **Informal:** Represented by unstated rules, how work gets done, and what it takes to succeed and fit into and have an organization value you

The work culture, both formal and informal, influences the way employees perform and interact with each other as employees and function as part of an organization. An organization is said to have a strong work culture when the majority of employees follow certain practices, beliefs, and existing guidelines regarding how the organization or function conducts itself and performs.

What is the strongest influence on an organization's work culture? The answer is leadership. Most workplaces reflect the personality and management style of its leadership. Leadership consciously or unconsciously has the greatest influence. This influence takes many forms: what is communicated, what employees are held accountable for, what the organization's values are, what is rewarded or reinforced, and of great importance, what example leadership is setting. However, employees need to buy in to the culture, which is a big part of reengaging employees or maintaining a highly engaged culture.

The real question is this:

> *Does leadership just allow culture to happen, or does it take an active, intentional role in creating the kind of culture that encourages all employees to be engaged?*

As a leader, you have the opportunity to influence those who call you their leader by what you say and do. You can instill a work culture even if it doesn't extend beyond those boundaries that you have the greatest opportunity to influence. The key is to become intentional regarding what you want the culture to be. You do this by:

- Being a positive role model for the kinds of beliefs, practices, customs, and behaviors *you want* shared by all employees
- Encouraging all employees to *understand and share* those same beliefs, practices, customs, and behaviors

> The key is to become intentional regarding what you want the culture to be.

Here, we put it all together into a model that illustrates how the various themes fit together:

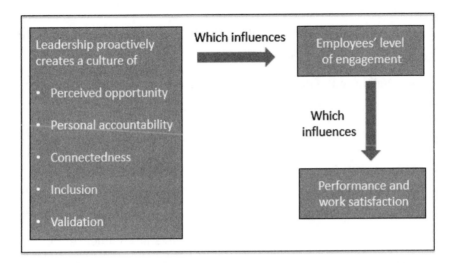

To increase or maintain high engagement, you, as the organization or function's leader, must proactively focus on how to infuse the five elements into your culture. The elements are as follows:

- **Perceived opportunity:** Engagement happens when employees feel they're part of something important and have something to believe in.

- **Personal accountability:** Engagement happens when employees are clear on what is expected of them and know why giving their best is important. When this is the case, personal accountability increases.

- **Connectedness:** Engagement happens when employees feel connected with each other, focus on mutual interest, and operate with shared responsibility. They create a collaborative mindset.

- **Inclusion:** Engagement happens when employees are well-informed and involved and when they have an opportunity to openly express their thoughts and feelings. In other words, people want to feel a part, which includes all aspects of the communication process.

- **Validation:** Engagement happens when employees feel they matter and have a valued place in the organization. Three elements of validation include support, recognition, and reward.

Through intentional practices, leaders begin to influence the employees' level of engagement. That in itself is significant, as research indicates. However, there is more. The elements also influence the performance and fulfillment or work satisfaction of your employees.

> A leader cannot make employees be engaged. A leader's role is to create the conditions under which people make the choice to be engaged.

What follows are a series of leader activities for each of the five elements. These activities focus on various practices available to you as a leader or as a leadership team where you collectively derive a plan of action for the organization. We introduce each of the elements and follow them with a series of activities that allow you to derive your plan of action.

Perceived opportunity

Element	Perceived opportunity
Premise	Engagement happens when employees feel they're part of something important and have something to believe in.
Significance	The mental energy that best serves full engagement is realistic optimism—working positively toward a desired future or outcome. Employees need to believe in the future. They need to see potential for giving the organization their energy. Having a *why* to work clearly increases engagement. Consequently, how you inform your employees is key to creating a culture of engagement.

Realistic optimism: Telling your story

How do you converse with the larger organization about the future in a manner that portrays current realities and at the same time provides hope or optimism for the future? The purpose of this activity is to develop a statement of realistic optimism that leads to buy-in regarding where the organization is going. Refer to chapter three for more information.

As a leader, answer the following questions:
- Regarding the future, what are you concerned or worried about? (Be transparent and realistic.)
- Regarding the future, what should employees be excited about?
- Why should employees stay and give their energy to where your function or where the organization is going?

Using the information from these questions, write a simple statement of realistic optimism that describes a positive picture about the future.

Developing your story

How you tell your story will have a significant impact on the energy of the organization. The Three Stories (see chapter three for more discussion) serves as a context to understand how often leaders describes their current reality.

The purpose of the activity is to identify how you use the attributes of Story Three to build what you want to focus on and achieve.

1. If you are in Story One or Story Two, first establish the reality of what your function or the organization is experiencing. Use any of the keywords that describe present conditions.
2. Create your story. Use some of the following attributes in a narrative that provides a picture of what you want your function or the organization to focus on or achieve:
   * How good can we get? Opportunity, collaboration, effectiveness, execution, growth, sustainability—add your own outcomes to this list.
3. Keep this story in front of your employees by using it as a vision or desired outcome. Engage others in determining how, together, you can make it happen.

Creating an organizing principle

Every organization consciously or unconsciously has an organizing principle that the entire function shares and drives how energy is used. Having an organizing principle gives those who call you their leader something to focus on and rally to.

An organizing principle (see chapter three) represents what you want employees to focus on or invest their energy in for the next twelve months. For example, if your thematic goal is quality, then you would organize around this principle by focusing on quality people, quality processes, quality standards, quality products, quality customer relationships, and quality operations. Refer to this illustration that appeared in chapter three:

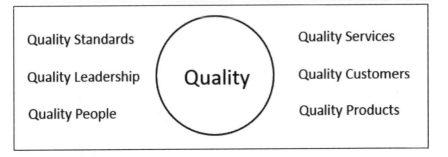

Quality Standards		Quality Services
Quality Leadership	**Quality**	Quality Customers
Quality People		Quality Products

The purpose of this activity is to identify your organizing principle, so you can begin to build what you want your employees to rally around.

1. Use the following questions to help decide your organizing principle:
   - What organizing principle is critical to helping us drive the mission/vision of the organization?
   - What organizing principle would get employees excited and engaged?
   - What organizing principle would give employees something to strive for?
   - What do we want our employees to think about and measure?
2. Place your organizing principle inside a circle on a sheet of paper.
3. Around the circle, write down the different ways you can organize around the principle (like the preceding quality example).
4. Determine how you'll organize and communicate this organizing principle to your employees.

Putting your story together

What do you need to do to enhance the element of perceived opportunity? Assume you're responsible for writing your organization's story—one that will engage your employees. Take into consideration the three key areas you have so far developed: realistic optimism, the Three Stories, and your operating principle.

---

1. What key elements from the three activities would you want to include in your organization's story that would reengage your employees?
2. Write your story as if you were speaking to the organization's larger constituency.

Personal accountability

Element	Personal accountability
Premise	Engagement happens when employees are clear on what is expected of them and know why it's important to give their best. When that's the case, personal accountability increases.
Significance	Employees, more often than not, tend to do what they believe is expected of them. If you want the best from employees, you need to expect the best. However, setting high expectations without accountability often leads to unfulfilled promise. When employees are clear about what is expected of them from both a performance goals and personal behavior perspective and know they'll be held accountable, they tend to hold themselves accountable. Therefore, personal accountability is often a stronger factor in an employee's engagement than the accountability that comes from external sources.

To develop a culture of personal accountability, you need to overtly articulate your expectations for employees and hold them accountable for fulfilling those expectations

Performance goals

The purpose of this application is to identify what you need to do to focus on performance goals, which we discussed in chapter four.

> Thinking of this from a leadership perspective, answer the following questions:
> - How are you currently holding management and employees accountable for their performance?
> - In the current organizational culture, what will need to change to more effectively build and use performance goals?
> - How can current processes for goal setting and performance management be used to more effectively enhance the use of performance goals?
> - As a leader, how can you instill and measure performance goals in your areas of responsibility?

Attaching expectations to organizational values

In today's corporate environment, most organizations have clearly stated values. However, not many have clearly stated behavioral expectations to accompany those values.

The purpose of this exercise is to attach behavioral expectations to your organizational values, which we discussed in greater detail in chapter four.

1.	List your organizational values.
2.	For each of the values you listed, identify the most critical behaviors required to demonstrate that value.
3.	Thinking of this from a leadership perspective, consider the following questions related to what you can do to create a culture of personal accountability: • What needs to be done to implement the previous values exercise so employees are clear on what is expected of them? • Beyond behavioral expectations attached to values, what other behavioral expectations do you want employees to adhere to? • How will you communicate these expectations to your employees? • How can current management processes be used to more effectively enhance the use of performance goals? • As a leader, how can you instill behavioral expectations in your areas of responsibility?

Connectedness

Element	Connectedness
Premise	Engagement happens when employees feel connected with each other, focus on mutual interest, and operate with shared responsibility. They create a collaborative mindset.
Significance	High-performing organizations will often point to their success by talking about their collaborative culture and the impact it has on productivity. There are two important aspects when it comes to employees' level of engagement: • **Trust and support:** Employees want to feel they're working with colleagues who trust and support each other and who demonstrate interest in not only their own success, but also in the success of their colleagues. Sustaining engagement is difficult when employees feel disconnected from their peers.

> • **Collaborative mindset:** Employees want to feel that their perspective counts, and leadership invites different perspectives and integrates them to accomplish a common outcome. As collaboration at all levels increases, so does connectedness and engagement increases.

Creating connections

The purpose of this activity is to identify what you as an individual leader can do to increase the connectedness of your key employees (refer to chapter five).

> Thinking of this from a leadership perspective, consider the following related to what you can do to increase the connectedness of your key employees:
> • Identify which of your key employees needs to be better connected to other key colleagues.
> • For each of those employees, identify the colleagues they should be better connected with.
> • For each of your key employees, identify what actions you could take to increase their connectedness with their colleagues.

Developing a collaborative mindset

High-performing organizations will often point to their success by talking about how they operate with a collaborative mindset, the process of integrating different functions or individual perspectives to accomplish a common outcome.

The purpose of this activity is to identify what you as an individual leader can do to increase the collaboration with and among your employees. This activity is best done in a discussion between you the leader and your employees.

Thinking of this from both a leadership perspective and an employee perspective, consider the following questions related to what you can do to increase the collaboration in your team:
- What do we currently do that exhibits good collaboration, and how can we continue to do those things?
- What barriers exist that might make collaborating difficult, and how can we remove or reduce them?
- What do we need to do differently or do more of to increase collaboration within our team?
- What are we committed to as the leader and as employees to improve collaboration?

Mutual influence and a collaborative culture

As a leader you play the most critical role in creating a collaborative culture first by practicing mutual influence skills, but also by creating the expectations that everyone has the skills to practice mutual influence. Head back to chapter five for more about mutual influence.

The purpose of this activity is to identify what you can do to implement the three skill sets that put mutual influence into practice.

Thinking from a leadership perspective, answer the following questions:
- What listening practices can I use to increase my effectiveness in the area of listen to learn?
- What listening practices can I use to increase my effectiveness in the area of express to explore?
- What listening practices can I use to increase my effectiveness in the area of integrate to innovate?

The Use of Teams: Chartering

Part of your job as a leader is to build connectedness with those people you lead, which may include your work team or your managers. The process is called *chartering,* which we discussed more in chapter five.

The purpose of this activity is to introduce a process that builds the big arrow and increases connectedness within work groups or teams. This activity is best done in a discussion between you, the leader, and your employees.

The following are the steps for you the leader to complete the chartering activity:
1. Identify your team and schedule a half to a full day to meet together.
2. Create a set of worksheets that reflect the questions the team needs to answer.

The process simply asks you to engage your team in answering the following questions:
- Whom do we serve? Who is our primary constituency and what do they require of us?
- Are there critical interfaces necessary to succeed?
- What is our desired outcome or purpose? How will the outcome benefit all team members and our constituents?
- What will success look like?
- What procedures will we need to put in place?
- What roles will individuals play?
- How will we relate to each other?

3. Use the results to guide the team moving forward.

Inclusion

Element	Inclusion
Premise	Engagement happens when employees are well-informed and involved and when they have an opportunity to openly express their thoughts and feelings. Simply stated, people want to feel a part, which includes all aspects of the communication process.
Significance	Inclusion naturally creates engagement. Suppressed communication naturally creates disengagement. How information is gathered, disseminated, and understood greatly impacts a sense of inclusion, as does whether individuals feel they have the freedom to openly express themselves. A lack of information flow is one of the fastest ways to create disengaged employees. If they don't feel included, they won't feel engaged.

Creating a culture of inclusion

How information is gathered, shared, disseminated, and understood greatly impacts the sense of inclusion as does whether individuals feel they have the freedom to openly express themselves. Refer to chapter six for more discussion on inclusion.

The purpose of this activity is to identify what the shared practices of the organization should be to increase trust and information flow.

Thinking of this from a leadership perspective, answer the following questions:

- Regarding the following, what are you currently doing well?
  - Involving people?
  - Information gathering and sharing?
  - Information systems?
  - Providing feedback?
- Regarding the following what do you need to change or do differently to improve?
  - Involving people?
  - Information gathering and sharing?
  - Information systems?
  - Providing feedback?

Encouraging people to step through the open door

What determines whether employees are willing to come through the open door as we discussed in chapter six? The reason is primarily the outcome of past interactions that have occurred between management and the employees.

So the question becomes: "What do leaders do consciously or unconsciously that decreases the level of trust, closes the open door, and diminishes the opportunity to experience a culture of inclusion?"

The purpose of this activity is to identify what you as a leader do that decreases the level of trust and what you can do to increase the level of trust.

Thinking of this from a leadership perspective, answer the following questions:
- Regarding the following behaviors, what are you currently doing that leads to low trust?
  - Judging
  - Expressing superiority
  - Being certain
  - Overcontrolling
  - Being indifferent
- Regarding the following, what do you need to do differently, or do more of, to exhibit behaviors that enhance trust?
  - Describing
  - Demonstrating equality
  - Being open
  - Empowering
  - Expressing interest

Validation

Element	Validation
Premise	Engagement happens when employees feel that they matter and that they have a valued place in the organization. Three elements of validation include support, development, and reward.
Significance	Validation is the expressed interest an organization has in its employees. It comes in a variety of forms: recognition, listening, involvement, understanding, rewards, learning, growth, and so on. Validation is arguably the most important element of engagement because it personally influences each individual in the organization. Showing interest is critical to retaining and engaging employees.

Acts of interest

Validation is demonstrating, as leaders, that you care about your employees' well-being, as we discussed in chapter seven. The best way to demonstrate caring is through acts of interest.

The purpose of this activity is to identify ways to validate your employees through acts of interest.

Thinking of this from a leadership perspective, answer this question:

What are the ways you could validate employees in the following areas?
- **Supporting** the individual as a person and for the work he or she does.
- **Rewarding** the individual with both monetary and natural rewards.
- **Developing** the individual by providing opportunities to learn and grow.

Using natural rewards to validate employees

Natural rewards aren't given for performance; they're something that a person finds intrinsically satisfying. The reward is built into the employee's daily work life. Natural rewards aren't the same for everyone. One employee may want to be rewarded by being given the opportunity to learn a new job, whereas another employee may want recognition. The key is discovering what is unique to each individual. Go to chapter seven for more information.

The purpose of this activity is to discover what natural rewards are important to your individual employees and consider how to provide those natural rewards.

1. Give your employees the natural rewards inventory and ask them to fill it out. Schedule some quality time to meet individually with them.
2. During the meeting with each employee, begin with some general questions:
   - What do you find rewarding about your work?
   - What would you love to have more time to do?
   - Have you had an opportunity to learn and grow over the last year?
3. Have the employee share with you what he or she selected as natural rewards in order of priority. For each reward, ask these questions:
   - Why is this reward important to you?
   - What can I do to help build that reward into your work?

Note: Often, you'll be able to accommodate the employee's requests. If you're unable to do so, explain why. Acknowledge the importance to the employee and suggest options. Even if no options are available, just having the conversation will likely make the employee feel better.

4. Identify which letters (M, C, P, LSC) were the most often chosen, and see if there are any themes to explore
5. Reach an agreement on what each of you will do to make each reward part of the employee's work.
6. Keep a record of your agreements so you can recall how to reward each employee uniquely.

Challenge	Acknowledgment	Team spirit
Frequently presented with the opportunity to create or complete challenging projects that provide achievement or accomplishment. M	Recognition of goals met or exemplary performance in work. Receiving credit when credit is due. Recognized by others for expertise. M	Being a valued member of the team. A positive, friendly, collaborative work culture that supports positive behaviors. C

Passion	Creativity	Informal environment
Having a reason to get up in the morning. Work allows you to deal with issues about which you have great interest, concern, and commitment. P	Opportunity to do work that requires new ways of doing things. Ability to take risks and get outside the box. M	Fun, enjoyable work environment where humor, laughter, and celebration regularly occur. Casual dress and relaxed atmosphere. C
Freedom Independence and autonomy. Ability to guide decisions regarding own projects. Opportunity to select work activities that make sense. LSC	**Self-expression** Encouraged and supported to fully express your talents. Recognized for individual aptitudes and unique qualities. M	**Contribution** Opportunity to have a direct impact on others and on the success of the organization. Make a lasting legacy. P
Meaning Opportunities to pursue a meaningful task. Strong sense of purpose or mission. Work worthy of time and energy. P	**Security** A job that isn't likely to be eliminated. Some assurance of career destiny and rewards. LSC	**Leadership** Confidence in leaders' abilities to anticipate and guide decisions or developing my leadership capacity and taking opportunities to lead. C
Workspace Healthy, positive work environment. Workspace conducive to productivity. Aesthetically pleasing space. LSC	**Mission** Work that helps people or improves things. The feeling that work contributes to ideals. P	**Courage** Support for bold ideas, a listening culture. Open dialogue encouraged. Easy to put hard issues on the table. C

Balance	Adventure	Clear feedback
Work leaves time for pursuits outside of work. Work activities honor family, community, and other pursuits. Lifestyle-friendly culture. LSC	Work environment provides situations with excitement and flair. Frequent risk-taking with possible loss or gain encouraged. LSC	The question, "How am I doing?" is clearly answered. Progress toward goals is noted and acknowledged. Positive feedback is given. M
Mentoring Opportunity to mentor the development of others or to be mentored by wise people. C	**Entrepreneurship** To engage in work that directly impacts success of a product or business. Receiving rewards through sense of invention or ownership. C	**Respect** Respected by colleagues and managers. Others seek opinions and ideas. C
Relationships Sense of belonging. Opportunity to develop close friendships. Frequent/open interpersonal contact. C	**Excellence** Be the best. Work allows for the pursuit of mastery, the development of new and existing capacities. Opportunities for development and learning encouraged. M	**Other** Create your own reward.

Epilogue

Looking Back

When we began, we set out to research how organizations lose their energy and provide insights on how as leaders, you can restore energy. Employee engagement, or more accurately, the lack of employee engagement was a hot topic with many studies indicating employee engagement was a continuing—if not worsening—problem. We believed then, as we do now, the bigger challenge is not how do you get employees engaged, but rather how you reengage employees who were once engaged, but have lost their energy. In our research, we quickly learned organizations could lose their energy in various ways, but two patterns of organizational change became clear.

One pattern had to do with significant, high impact change. Examples of this are mergers and acquisitions, major layoffs, or reallocations of resources to other facilities. What became clear to us was the role that perceived loss played in these types of events. The other pattern of change that cause organizations to lose their energy included ongoing, repetitive change leading to change fatigue or apathy, low job satisfaction, and arguably the most important, ineffective leadership. Leaders need to understand that their example (behavior and thinking) contributes to or

241

stands in the way of high engagement. As we said in chapter two, leaders either give energy or take energy away.

One of the other things we discovered is a good definition of the word *engagement* doesn't exist. We had hoped we might provide a strong working definition of what engagement entails. It doesn't mean high work satisfaction, which is often how the level of engagement is determined in surveys. Although important, engagement is the perception of what is being requested of them (negative, neutral, or positive) and how much energy they chose to expend on the request. Therefore, engagement occurs when the perception of what is happening is positive and the choice is to provide discretionary energy to it. The importance of this definition is made clear when you realize the role leadership can play in influencing both perception and choice.

Regardless of the type of change occurring in the organization, leaders need to understand the critical role that they play in the choice that employees make about whether to be engaged or not. We wanted our readers to understand you can reengage an organization by having leadership focus on five key elements that contribute most to restoring employee satisfaction and energy:

- **Perceived opportunity:** Creating a culture of realistic optimism by how you tell your story.
- **Personal accountability:** Establishing personal accountability regarding both performance and behavior.
- **Inclusion:** Practicing inclusion based on trust.
- **Connectedness:** Making connections by creating a collaborative environment.

- **Validation:** Demonstrating you care by placing a high level of emphasis on recognizing, developing, and supporting employees.

Our third objective was to provide applications and tools that guide an organization's leadership in applying the five key elements. It isn't enough to tell leaders where to focus; we need to help them understand what to do.

With employee engagement being such a hot topic, along the way we often have heard people say that there already were numerous books on engagement, so why another one? We truly believe this book brings a fresh perspective with new insights and tools. We sent our draft manuscript to a variety of corporate readers representing large, medium, and small corporations; leaders who had experienced the disengagement of their workforce were frustrated with initiatives that failed to render any lasting results. They thanked us for a book that provided content they could apply that clearly provided a set of strategies they could follow. One of the individuals who read the book even asked if Nancy from Avcor was actually him that we were talking about. That reaction, although slightly amusing, reflects what many leaders are going though and how closely they can identify with the challenges we described. Today, organizations still need insight and help with the challenges of how to reengage employees who were once engaged and energized. We hope the book has proved its relevance to you as well.

Now that we are at our journey's end, it occurs to us that we learned so much from each other as we worked on the book. At times we talked through an idea or approach and together came up with a better expression of our thinking than we could have had as individuals. We want to summarize by using some of the boxed points of emphasis throughout our book as some of the key insights we hope you will remember as you journey through the challenges of organizational life:

- The way energy is used is the currency of engagement.
- Leaders either give energy or take energy out of the organization.
- Engagement: positive perception, high discretionary energy.
- In essence, the role of leadership is to influence how employees perceive the impact of change on the organization and how employees use their energy.
- The next time your organization is about to experience change, ask yourself, "How are employees likely to experience gain or loss?"
- The greater the perceived loss, the greater the likelihood of disengagement.
- Employees who are experiencing the death of ambition use their energy to remain undiscovered.
- Ultimately a leader won't be judged so much by how he or she led, but how well he or she was followed.
- The question for leaders to answer is, "Where do you get your signals from that influence and shape you as a leader: from the inside (essence) or the outside (form)?"
- Leadership is the ability to take others to a place they wouldn't go by themselves, not by the power of the leader's position, but by the strength of the leader's example.
- My ability to influence you is directly tied to my willingness to be influenced by you.

- A key to reengagement is to establish a positive and realistic "belief" in the future—a perceived opportunity.

- The ability to hold oneself accountable, and monitor one's own performance, is a stronger factor in an employee's reengagement than if accountability and feedback on performance comes from external sources such as a manager.

- As collaboration at all levels increases, so does connectedness, and engagement increases.

- Don't pride yourself on having an open door policy. Pride yourself on the number of people who come through your door.

- The key element that had the greatest impact was both simple and profound: A demonstrated interest in the employee by his or her manager.

One thing we have learned by working with a variety of organizations is the basic reality that organizations disengage quickly, but reengagement is a long-term, culture-changing process. We couldn't leave you without answering the question, "What happened to Avcor?" Although we never had the opportunity to work to restore engagement with Avcor Technologies, their story continues. Yet another company with a new leadership team who is trying hard to recapture the energy that had been lost previously acquired Avcor. Maybe the most important thing they have done is to restore a sense of perceived opportunity by focusing on realistic optimism and by helping the employees see they have an important role to play in the organization's future. The new leadership team is also aware of the fact that change is and will continue to impact the organization, so increasing the inclusion of the employees in the change process is critical. Although the organization is much smaller than it once was, it seems to be moving past just surviving and beginning to focus again on its potential to grow.

We wish you well on your own journey and may your organization thrive and produce the most engaged, fulfilled, contributory individuals possible.

Steve Buchholz and Tom Roth

References

Ainsworth-Land, George. *Grow or Die: The Unifying Principle of Transformation.* New York: John Wiley & Sons, 1986.

Bennis, Warren and Nanus, Burt. *Leaders: Strategies for Taking Charge.* New York: Harper & Row, 1985.

Blum, Arlene. *Breaking Trail: A Climbing Life.* New York: Scribner, 2005.

Buchholz, Steve and Roth, Thomas. *Creating the High Performance Team.* New York: John Wiley & Sons, 1987.

Buchholz, Steve and Woodward, Harry. *Aftershock: Helping People through Corporate Change.* New York: John Wiley & Sons, 1987.

Buford, Bob. *Half Time: Changing Your Game Plan from Success to Significance.* Grand Rapids: Zondervan, 1994.

Cashman, Kevin. *Leadership from the Inside Out: Becoming a Leader for Life.* San Francisco: Berrett-Koehler, 1998.

Cohen, Daniel I.A. and Bradford, David. *Managing for Excellence: The Guide to Developing High Performance in Contemporary Organizations.* New York: John Wiley & Sons, 1984.

Connor, Daryl R. *Managing at the Speed of Change: How Resilient Mangers Succeed and Prosper Where Others Fail.* New York: Random House, 1992.

Covey, Stephen M.R. and Merrill, Rebecca. *The Speed of Trust: The One Thing That Changes Everything.* New York: Free Press, 2006.

Deal, Terrence E. and Kennedy, Allen A. *Corporate Cultures: The Rites and Rituals of Corporate Life.* Reading, MA: Addison-Wesley, 1996. *Leading Change.* Boston: Harvard Business School Press, 1982.

George, Bill and Sims, Peter. *True North: Discover Your Authentic Leadership.* San Francisco: Jossey-Bass, 2007.

Gibb, Jack R. *Trust: A New View of Personal and Organizational Development.* San Francisco: Astron Series Book, 1978.

Greenleaf, Robert K. *The Power of Servant Leadership.* San Francisco: Berrett-Koehler Publishers, 1998.

Herzberg, Fredrick; Mausner Bernard; and Snyderman, Barbara Bloch. *The Motivation to Work.* New Brunswick: Transaction Publishers, 1959.

Helgesen, Sally. *The Web of Inclusion*. New York: Currency/Doubleday, 1995.

Kay, Beverly and Evens-Jordan, Sharon. *Love 'Em or Lose' Em: Getting Good People to Stay*. San Francisco: Barrett-Koehler, 1999

Kotter, John P. *Leading Change: An Action Plan from the Foremost Expert on Business Leadership*. Boston: Harvard Business Review Press, 1996,

Leath, Blake. *Cultivating the Strategic Mind: Growing from Leader to Visionary, Creator, and Architect of Strategy*. Indianapolis: IBJ Book Publishing, LLC, 2017.

Leider, Richard J. *The Power of Purpose: Creating Meaning in Your Life and Work*. New York: Fawcett, 1985.

Loer, J and Schwartz, Tony. *The Power of Full Engagement: Managing Energy, Not Time, Is the Key to High Performance and Personal Renewal*. New York: Free Press, 2003.

Maslach, Christina. *Burnout: The Cost of Caring*. Cambridge: Malor Books, 1982.

Maslach, Christina and Jackson, Susan. *Burnout Inventory: The Leading Measure of Burnout*. Cambridge: Malor Books, 1981.

Noer, David M. *Healing the Wounds: Overcoming the Trauma of Layoffs and Revitalizing Downsized Organizations*. San Francisco: Jossey-Bass Publishers, 1993

Elop, Stephen CEO. Feb. 9, 2011. Posted to an internal Nokia employee system and reported in *The Guardian*.

Oshry, Barry. *Seeing Systems: Unlocking the Mysteries of Organizational Life*. San Francisco: Berrett-Koehler Publishers, 1995.

Senge, Peter. *The Fifth Discipline: The Art and Practice of the Learning Organization*. New York: Currency/Doubleday, 1990.

Sinek, Simon. *Start with the Why: How Great Leaders Inspire Everyone to Take Action*. New York: Portfolio, 2009.

Tichy, Noel M. and Devanna, M.A. *The Transformational Leader*. New York: John Wiley & Sons, 1986.

Tichy, Noel M. and Ulrich, David O. "SMR Forum: *The Leadership Challenge—A Call for the* Transformational Leader." *Sloan Management Review,* Fall 1984, pp. 59-68.

Tillich, P. *The Courage to Be*. New Haven, Conn: Yale University Press, 1952.

Vaill, Peter B. *Managing as A Performing Art: New Ideas For A World Of Chaotic Change*. San Francisco: Jossey-Bass, 1989.

Woodward, Harry L. and Tager, Mark J. *Leadership in Times of Stress and Change: Seven Skills for Gaining Trust and Inspiring Confidence.* La Jolla: Work Skills-Life Skills, 2002.

Author Biographies

Dr. Steve Buchholz

Dr. Steve Buchholz is a recognized leader in the field of change management. Along with Harry Woodward, Steve authored the business best seller, Aftershock: Helping People Through Corporate Change. Steve has also written The Positive Manager, and co-authored with Tom Roth, Creating the High Performance Team. He holds a doctorate in Organizational Sociology from the University of Nebraska.

Steve works with a variety of companies focusing on leadership capacity, high performance teaming, mobilizing the energy of the organization (change management), talent retention, engagement, and developing strategic alignment.

A special part of his work has become one-on one coaching, helping individuals re-find their smile, discover their potential, and move to mastery.

Mr. Tom Roth

Mr. Tom Roth is Chief Operating Officer for Wilson Learning Worldwide and President of Wilson Learning Worldwide Japan. As such, he is responsible for the strategic direction and business performance of

Wilson Learning Worldwide operations. He assists global executive leadership teams with issues related to employee engagement, leadership development, strategy alignment, and business transformation.

Mr. Roth has spent over 35 years developing and implementing human performance improvement solutions. He and Steve Buchholz co-authored the book Creating the High Performance Team and is a frequent speaker at national and international conferences. He speaks on a variety of issues, including leadership, employee and customer engagement, change, and strategy implementation. He is published in numerous business publications.

Endorsements

Unplugged is an important overview and reference guide for any leader who cares about working in teams and managing people for top performance. It will join a select few business books that are well worn, read and reread as leaders encounter new situations and want to remind themselves of the fundamentals.

Dr. Sarah Kelly head of Pharmaceutical Sciences Small Molecule,
Pfizer Worldwide Research and Development

'Unplugged' is the culmination of numerous progressive management programs and techniques that helped guide us through business cycles to continuous success. An excellent, concise reference book, well written with relatable examples.

Andy Fulton, President, ME Global Inc

Working with Dr. Steve Buchholz as a mentor and CEO coach for over two decades, I have learned the necessity of having a fully engaged workforce to successfully drive the business. Without a highly engaged work culture, our business stagnated, and with it, the business flourished with its greatest years of growth and profitability and, being recognized as a "Best Place to Work" for 8 consecutive years. Every business leader and CEO needs to heed the invaluable advice of the authors in this book for the only way to create true sustainable success.

Joe Grabowski, CEO – Retired Wenck Enterprises, Inc

In Unplugged, Buchholz and Roth clarify why and how organizations lose the energy of their people, and what leaders must do to reengage their employees. The authors also define the key features of essence-based leadership which contribute to establishing a coherent and united culture. If you are waiting for wise advice on how to preserve the emotional engagement inside your organization, add value to your clients, and build sustainability and differentiation, this is the right book for you.

Alberto Pérez La Rotta, author of Integrated Business Transformation